CONTEMPORARY
BOTANICAL
ARTISTS

THE SHIRLEY SHERWOOD COLLECTION

For Jay and Judy,
Supporters of the
'Botanical':
Katherine .

Josephine Hague

CONTEMPORARY BOTANICAL ARTISTS

THE SHIRLEY SHERWOOD COLLECTION

BY SHIRLEY SHERWOOD

EDITED BY VICTORIA MATTHEWS

CELEBRATING THE RENAISSANCE OF BOTANICAL ART

WITH WORK COLLECTED DURING THE LAST FIVE YEARS

FROM OVER A HUNDRED PAINTERS, LIVING IN

SEVENTEEN DIFFERENT COUNTRIES

AROUND THE WORLD.

WEIDENFELD & NICOLSON

IN ASSOCIATION WITH

THE ROYAL BOTANIC GARDENS, KEW

First published in Great Britain in 1996 by
George Weidenfeld & Nicolson Ltd

Weidenfeld and Nicolson Ltd
The Orion Publishing Group
Orion House
5 Upper St Martin's Lane
London WC2H 9EA

A catalogue record for this book is available from the British Library

ISBN 0 279 836005

Book design by Harry Green
Printed and bound in Great Britain by
Butler & Tanner Ltd, Frome and London

JACKET ILLUSTRATIONS
Front: Blue Water Lily by Pandora Sellars
Details left to right: Artichokes by Brigid Edwards; Bromeliad by
Margaret Mee; Ginkgo by Tai-li Zhang; Camellia by Paul Jones;
Rhododendron by Sally Kier; Begonia by Ann Farrer
Back: Pansies by Susannah Blaxill

Frontispiece
CLEMATIS ELSA SPATH
Josephine Hague, 1991

CONTENTS

EXHIBITION VENUES

KEW GARDENS GALLERY
Royal Botanic Gardens, Kew, Richmond, Surrey

THE HUNT INSTITUTE FOR BOTANICAL DOCUMENTATION
Carnegie Mellon University, Pittsburgh, Pennsylvania

WAVE HILL
at The National Arts Club, 15 Gramercy Park South
New York, NY 10003

FOREWORDS

Botanical art has always played an important part in the programme of the Royal Botanic Gardens, Kew. Part of our large collection of botanical art has come from our long association with *Curtis's Botanical Magazine,* the oldest continually published journal with colour illustrations of plants. In 1988 we opened the Kew Gardens Gallery to promote the work of contemporary artists, as well as to display some of our great collection of botanical art.

We were most pleased when our gallery stimulated Dr Shirley Sherwood to start collecting the work of contemporary artists. She has chosen some of the best work of each of the artists who have exhibited in the Kew Gardens Gallery, and has built up a fascinating and important collection. This has been an encouragement to many of the finest botanical artists of today. I am most pleased that we are now able to exhibit her fine collection in the gallery. The Kew Gardens Gallery has helped stimulate and revive interest and encourage a high quality of botanical art and this exhibition helps us to continue this fine tradition.

PROFESSOR SIR GHILLEAN PRANCE
Director
Royal Botanic Gardens, Kew

Dr Sherwood's collection, housed in England and undoubtedly the finest of contemporary botanical art in private hands, has been assembled within just the past five years. This remarkable feat is due not solely to her background as a biologist, or her opportunities for extensive travel, but to a discerning eye and a passion to seek out only the finest contemporary painters in order to acquire examples by each. With this exhibition she hopes to introduce these artists to a wider public and to continue to bring this genre out of museums' ancillary collections and into their main salons.

The idea for this exhibition arose spontaneously among Brinsley Burbidge, Victoria Matthews and myself, following luncheon in the Sherwoods' orangery at their country home, Hinton, two years ago. Dr Sherwood was enthusiastic about the idea and has shown great zeal in setting up the exhibition at Kew, and in the United States, as well as seeing to all details of this accompanying book. The results of her efforts have made a distinctive mark indeed.

JAMES J. WHITE
Curator of Art and Principal Research Scholar
Hunt Institute for Botanical Documentation
Carnegie Mellon University, Pittsburgh, Pennsylvania

THE SHIRLEY SHERWOOD COLLECTION OF BOTANICAL ILLUSTRATION

DR BRINSLEY BURBIDGE

The Shirley Sherwood Collection is unique. Rarely has such an important and fascinating cross-section of what was going on in a single field of creative activity at one time, worldwide, been brought together in one place. Almost never has the energy of a single highly knowledgeable collector of impeccable discrimination been brought to bear on a group of artists who are linked only by the subject of their art or craft and who, through magazines and other publications, are only remotely aware of one another's work.

The collection is a lot more than the documentation of the work produced by a few artists working at a particular time. It is first and foremost a supremely beautiful selection of paintings. The plants themselves contribute significantly to this beauty but the artists chosen by Dr Sherwood have, in almost every case, elevated what could so easily have been a representational painting into a real work of art in which composition, use of colour, and skill in the handling of paint have combined to create works of true beauty. Many of the paintings give a new perspective on the plants themselves, many are so stunningly lifelike that one is drawn to look closely at them and marvel at the sheer skill of the painters.

This collection also tells us so much: it tells us about the process of botanical illustration, how it is done and what the scientist needs in a painting of a plant. It reinforces the fact that, even in the face of instantaneous and accurate photography, botanical painters are still in demand and can satisfy the need for scientific precision more adeptly than can any camera. It shows how, in an age of easy communication, national styles persist and the influence of one painter on another can be traced. It shows that there is still room for the artist in the service of science and fills us with surprise at the number of craftsmen-illustrators throughout the world who are able to make a living (not usually a generous one) from this exacting craft.

My first meeting with Dr Shirley Sherwood was just over five years ago when I had helped to start a gallery at the Royal Botanic Gardens, Kew. Its purpose was to display the best of historical and contemporary botanical painting. Dr Sherwood, as editor of the *Illustrated London News*, asked me to write an article on the subject. I took the opportunity to show my usual enthusiasm for it and also showed her some original paintings from the Kew collection. She was hooked. That moment was, for me, the beginning of a great relationship with someone who would do more for contemporary botanical painting than I could ever do through gallery exhibitions.

From the time of her first purchase of a work by Pandora Sellars, Dr Sherwood relentlessly pursued the acquisition of great paintings by the finest living botanical artists. She bought from galleries and, once she got to know the artists, commissioned them to fill specific gaps in the collection. One thing distinguished everything she selected: quality. Dr Sherwood unerringly went for the most important or the most innovative picture in any exhibition and, although this is another way of saying that I agree with her, she showed impeccable discrimination in choosing what she ultimately bought and added to her collection.

The collection rapidly grew in significance and very soon began to take on a life of its own in which a gap soon became evident: some significant painters were obviously missing. To tell the whole story, works by specific painters would have to be sought out and added. See, for example, Dr Sherwood's unfailing pursuit of paintings by Thalia Lincoln, Rory McEwen (one of the few non-living artists represented) or Celia Rosser. What was significant and most impressive about this process of adding new pictures was that no distance was too great and no location too obscure for her to go in search of an artist of note. No time was too long to wait for a commission to come to fruition and few artists were too aloof to succumb to Dr Sherwood's persistence in adding their work to her increasingly comprehensive collection. Most collections of botanical paintings come from a limited area of the globe but hers is truly international, with representation from all the countries where an active tradition of illustration exists.

As the collection grew, so did Dr Sherwood's contacts with, and knowledge of, new and exciting artists with the result that she was now telling me of painters of whom I should take notice. Her influence spread and in 1995 the works of some twenty or more artists were included in the 8th International Exhibition at the Hunt Institute for Botanical Documentation in Pittsburgh, partly as a result of her direct recommendation.

By 1994, the collection had so increased in size and significance that it began to attract scholars interested in seeing the works of important botanical painters; a visit to the Sherwood's house at Hinton near Oxford was a vital pilgrimage for anyone interested in plant illustration. Hinton, very much a one-stop-shop for world botanical art, is a lovely house and a perfect setting in which the paintings are beautifully mounted, framed and displayed. A day spent there looking at so many outstanding pictures is a day to remember.

The importance of the collection demanded that it should be more widely known and two years ago, on a visit to Hinton with James White of the Hunt Institute and Vicki Matthews, the idea was conceived that there should be a travelling exhibition. One of my last acts at Kew before I left for Florida was to discuss with Dr Sherwood the possibility of producing a book which would serve as a catalogue but also stand in its own right. Happily, both the exhibition and the book have happened and the collection can now be shared with everyone who is interested.

Let us look in a little more depth at its importance, not as documentation of what happened but as a starting point for some future activities; and let us consider it in the context of what has happened in botanical illustration in recent years.

Botanical painting will always be needed as a way of recording plants both for scientific study and for identification. The superiority of identification guides which use paintings over those illustrated with photographs is immediately obvious. The fact that a skilled artist, working together with a botanist, can show all the significant features which aid accurate identification gives illustration an insurmountable advantage. This alone ensures that there will always be work for botanical painters. The introduction of new means of communication will not reduce the importance of the picture. The tradition is strong and classes in botanical illustration continue to be popular, as does scientific illustration, as a college course. I have been present at many of these courses and taken part in informal discussions among the aspiring artists. The conversation almost invariably concentrates on technique and nothing enlivens that discussion more than an original painting by a master of the craft.

This is where the Shirley Sherwood Collection can have its greatest influence. Those painters who are fortunate enough to see the paintings whenever and wherever they are exhibited will derive an enormous amount of inspiration from them. Here, technique in the representation of a specific subject is at its very finest. Nowhere else are so many examples of a craft brought together for close inspection. And here is the answer to the question: I wonder how he/she did that? The superb reproductions in this book are almost as good as the originals. Dr Sherwood has chosen to show details from many of the paintings and these can be used to study how the artist handles paint.

I hope the collection will also inspire those who do not paint to have a try. The sheer quality of the works should stimulate inspiration but it can, I believe, also be a disincentive: how can I ever be as good as that? Even some of the leading botanical artists have such thoughts and self-questioning but the persistence to overcome doubt is a healthy process. I hope it will also stimulate the purchase of pictures, for here is a modest art with comparatively modest prices. It is not difficult to acquire a good collection without spending a fortune: the problem is the widely scattered nature of the sources of good paintings.

Let me draw this brief note together with some general and personal observations on botanical illustration. When, some 35 years ago, I first took an interest in the subject – inspired by the publication of Wilfrid Blunt's wonderful and scholarly *The art of botanical illustration*, it was extraordinarily difficult to see good work and botanical artists laboured, unappreciated, in dusty corners of museums and botanical garden herbaria. Their often beautiful work went straight into folders and was seen only by a small number of dedicated botanists. I was one of those dedicated botanists and spent time in places such as the Natural History Museum in London or the Fitzwilliam Museum in Cambridge looking at the paintings when I should have been looking at plants.

I did everything I could to give more publicity to botanical illustration by means of talks, classes and exhibitions. With Elizabeth Blackadder, I started a botanical painting course at the Edinburgh College of Art and, as mentioned earlier, I helped to start a gallery devoted to botanical art at Kew. At the same time the Hunt Institute for Botanical Documentation did a wonderful job of showing, on a regular basis, some really fine historical and contemporary work. There was a handful of similarly enthusiastic supporters 'out there' and between us we encouraged this fragile art until, by the later 1980s, the network of painters and collectors was well established and the Society of Botanical Artists, based in the United Kingdom, came into being – followed more recently by the American Society of Botanical Artists.

The result of all this activity was that the quality of work and the calibre of those drawn to botanical illustration increased dramatically until, as I write this introduction, I believe that I can say that the best works being produced today are the equal of, and often surpass, anything which has gone before. Redouté, Ehret and the Bauer brothers have their rightful place in the pantheon of great contributors to the art but beside them are many of the artists represented in the Shirley Sherwood Collection.

Here we have something truly wonderful; a collection which documents not only a particular period in the development of a craft but which also sets a standard for the future. I cannot imagine work even finer than that shown here – but I suspect that someone said exactly these words at Kew in the middle of the last century. I said them in the early 1970s once I had seen the work of Franz and Ferdinand Bauer.

This collection has proved me wrong.

In conclusion, I feel we are at the door of a new era in the practice and appreciation of scientific illustration. Recent prices paid at auction for illustrated natural history books show that there is an appreciative audience. The supply of these important historical books is limited but the supply of botanical paintings that are equal to, or better than, anything which has gone before continues. The first public viewing of the Shirley Sherwood Collection will give added impetus to artists to produce something even better and will help to maintain the supremely high standards set in recent years.

Botanical illustration always had an assured future based on need: art in the service of science. Thanks to the Shirley Sherwood Collection it now has a future in the public eye.

ON COLLECTING

SHIRLEY SHERWOOD

Looking back to the start of this collection, in July 1990, I realize how important my very first purchase was and what a wonderful choice I made. It was an orchid painted by Pandora Sellars, set in a tropical wonderland. After that initial plunge I became more and more interested, indeed obsessed, tracking down artists in far-flung countries as I realized that there was a great renaissance in botanical painting and that it was indeed a worldwide phenomenon.

In fact my interests were engaged many years earlier, when I was a child. I remember deciding at nine years old, as I watched my mother drawing in her studio, that I would become a flower painter. By the age of fourteen I was collecting in the Himalaya, and took my dried specimens rather nervously to the Herbarium at the Royal Botanic Gardens at Kew where my amateur offerings were gracefully accepted. Another important moment came when I was given Wilfrid Blunt's seminal reference book *The art of botanical illustration* as a prize just before I left school. I went on to read botany at Oxford, the only woman botanist in the whole university that year.

It was immediately after Oxford that my career in botany faltered. I had intended to train as a botanical illustrator, but I became increasingly disconcerted as I realized how few illustrators even managed to get their names in print. I was enthusiastic and impatient and not sure that I was designed for what seemed a back-room existence, however rewarding it might be. So I moved to the laboratory next door to the Oxford Botany School and started medically orientated research. This culminated in working with Sir James Black who led the team which discovered Tagamet, one of the most successsful drugs ever produced, which has been used to treat millions of people for duodenal ulcers. Later he was awarded the Nobel Prize for this discovery. It was a challenging and sometimes exhausting part of my life, but very satisfying.

During that time I had a year's 'sabbatical' leave and visited Australia where I became fascinated by the extraordinary native plants and started visiting botanical gardens again. Looking back I realize that two of 'my' artists, Celia Rosser and Paul Jones, were actively painting there at the time, but I never saw their work.

In 1977 I married James Sherwood and embarked on a completely different way of life, travelling all over the world to visit ports, container factories and luxury hotels. My husband is the president of Sea Containers and is probably best known for reviving the Orient-Express train service across Europe and owning a number of exclusive and unusual hotels. I became intrigued with the restoration of the Orient-Express and eventually wrote a book about it. I started two new publications, the *Orient-Express Magazine* and the *Eastern & Oriental Magazine*, and helped to edit the *Illustrated London News*.

In a curious way it was the *Orient-Express Magazine* that brought my botanical interests full circle again. In 1988 I heard Dr Brinsley Burbidge lecture on botanical illustration at the Royal Horticultural Society in London. I thought it was a fascinating subject which would make a wonderful article so I tracked him down at the Royal Botanic Gardens, Kew, and commissioned him to write a piece entitled 'Botanical Theatre' for the *Orient-Express Magazine* and the *Illustrated London News*. Brinsley Burbidge encouraged me to become involved with Kew which had just appointed a new director, Professor Ghillean Prance. The Kew Gardens Gallery had recently opened and was holding a series of exhibitions initiated by Brinsley, designed to show off the works of the best botanical artists of the day. One of its first shows featured over 60 of Margaret Mee's strong flower portraits to mark the publication of her book *In search of flowers of the Amazon forests*. Sadly, I missed meeting that remarkable, intrepid woman who made 15 challenging trips into the Amazon in search of rare and beautiful plants, but died in a car accident just after the exhibition.

I became a trustee of Kew's new Foundation, an organization designed to raise funds for Kew as well as to raise its profile. I decided that I could help further by becoming a patron of the new Kew Gardens Gallery. Little did I realize that I was embarking on an entirely new passion that would occupy so much of my time and energy over the next five years.

In the beginning I bought, rather cautiously, from the gallery but soon I was looking out for artists on my travels and beginning to trust my own judgement. I quickly realized that there were some painters of particular importance who should be represented in a definitive collection of contemporary botanical artists. Margaret Mee had, of course, greatly influenced a whole generation of environmentalists, alerting them to the dangerous exploitation of the Amazon through her paintings of tropical plants. Pandora Sellars has created 'botanical theatre' with her wonderfully executed compositions, while Brigid Edwards has painted especially luminous, arresting studies on vellum. Rory McEwen had taken the traditional way of painting flowers a number of steps beyond botanical illustration into the realm of modern art and had considerable influence on some contemporary painters while doing so. I was able to acquire work by Margaret Mee, Paul Jones, Raymond Booth and Pandora Sellars early on, but some artists were hard to come by. I have only just recently received Celia Rosser's superb 'Banksia', which took her four months to paint, and managed to acquire Rory McEwen's 'Summer 1974. Old Fashioned Rose, Beech Mast and Clover' from his estate only just in time for inclusion here.

My first important overseas acquisitions were in Rio de Janeiro, where I bought several of Margaret Mee's early paintings; and it was also in Brazil that I first discovered the existence of the Hunt Institute for Botanical Documentation at Pittsburgh, USA. The Hunt is a well-kept secret in Europe – and, indeed, very few Americans have heard of it unless they are professional botanists or illustrators. The Demonte family near Rio, all passionate naturalists, told me about this splendid academic institution which had given them a memorable exhibition. It stands on Carnegie Mellon campus, housed in a large, square building with two floors containing its extensive library and collection of pictures and prints. The top floor accommodates a gallery for exhibitions and a rare books room designed by Rachel Hunt who, during her lifetime, created a truly wonderful collection of books and paintings which has been much expanded since then. She and her husband founded and endowed the institute in 1960. One of its most important roles has been to hold international exhibitions every three or four years which show one or two works by selected artists from all over the world. The recent catalogues, edited by James White, the curator of art, have an invaluable list of the artists' names, addresses and curricula vitae. The 7th International Exhibition was held in 1992 and when I visited it I immediately realized that they provided an unrivalled source for contacting illustrators on my travels. In 1993 Jim White, Brinsley Burbidge and Brinsley's wife, the botanical editor Vicki Matthews, came to Hinton to see my growing collection. Jim and Brinsley immediately suggested that we could put together an exhibition to be shown at Kew and later at the Hunt. Little did I realize at the time quite what was entailed.

Helped by the Hunt catalogues and my growing list of contacts, and by friends who knew of my obsession, I arranged to visit galleries and artists in the their studios all over the world. 'Studio' is sometimes a rather grandiose name for the artist's workplace: often it was a converted bedroom, study or even part of a kitchen. Often, too, there was almost nothing to see: botanical painters work slowly and painstakingly, selling everything as soon as it is finished. A few of them are confident, vigorous, outgoing characters, but many are rather shy, quiet individuals who work long hours alone, seeking a perfection and precision which is barely appreciated in the outside world.

In some countries it was particularly difficult to meet artists. I found communication in Japan and China complicated as so few of the illustrators speak or write English. Fortunately, I have a great friend in Keiko Saino who was an invaluable interpreter when I communicated with the Japanese artists. Literally thousands of people in Japan paint flowers, many to the highest botanical and artistic standards. In general their work tends to follow the

Western tradition rather than being pronouncedly Japanese in character. Superb exhibitions are held in department stores and offices and there is a huge annual show in the Natural Science Museum, Tokyo, for which several thousand schoolchildren and their teachers submit illustrations for a final selection of some two hundred paintings.

Some of the world's most outstanding botanical artists live in Australia. Paul Jones' wonderful flower portraits are probably the best known worldwide, while Celia Rosser's inspired, meticulous work reproduced in *The banksias* is famous for its perfect merging of the arts and sciences. Susannah Blaxill's arresting watercolours are enthusiastically collected in London while Jenny Phillips' lovely studies are admired by patrons and students alike. Jenny runs an active school for would-be botanical painters and has taught over three hundred people in a recent two-year period. I was enormously impressed by the standard and enthusiasm on a recent visit to her class in Melbourne.

Teaching botanical art is a growth industry these days. The classes at Kew are full, the English Gardening School at London's Chelsea Physic Garden is running successful courses under the expert guidance of Ann Marie Evans, and Margaret Mee scholars arrive from Brazil each year for several months' tuition with Christabel King and Annie Farrer. Interest is also burgeoning in North America, with Pamela Stagg teaching in Toronto, Linda Funk in Maine and Katie Lee near New York, to mention only a few. The newly formed American Society of Botanical Artists is further indication of rising interest.

South Africa is another 'cluster spot' for painters. This is really not surprising as the unique flora of the Cape of Good Hope is particularly outstanding. The National Botanical Institutes at Pretoria and at Kirstenbosch in Cape Town have encouraged artists to work with their scientists, resulting in some beautifully illustrated books. With the isolation induced by apartheid many South African illustrators are hardly known outside their own country, but Ellaphie Ward-Hilhorst and Thalia Lincoln have certainly received international recognition.

Certain galleries and institutions around the world have encouraged this upsurge of interest in botanical art. In London the Tryon Gallery, Spink, David Ker, Jonathan Cooper's Park Walk Gallery, the English Gardening School and, above all, Kew Gardens Gallery, have held interesting exhibitions in the last few years. A number of fine art galleries are beginning to show this type of work rather successfully. Brigid Edwards' recent exhibition in Old Bond Street, London, was completely sold out before the doors even opened for the private view. The Royal Horticultural Society (RHS) in London exhibits works by about 20 contemporary botanical artists at the Westminster Shows, Vincent Square, London, during the four mid-winter months and awards a number of highly prized medals. The compulsory eight entries submitted by each artist are judged for their scientific accuracy as well as their artistic merit. There are usually a number of entries from abroad and the standard can be extremely high. A large proportion of the artists whose works are in my collection have been awarded gold or silver medals and I have sometimes first made contact with them at the society meetings. The RHS's Lindley Library occasionally adds to its wonderful collection from these exhibitions. The Society of Botanical Artists (SBA) has a large annual show of members' work at the Westminster Central Hall, London. The Hunt Institute is a vital focal point in the United States, as is the Everard Read Gallery in Johannesburg.

Most of the works in my collection are by United Kingdom illustrators. This is not only because I live mostly in London and so have more time to seek out local artists. The fact is that the English and Scots have always had a tradition for painting flowers and a passionate interest in their gardens. Today this enthusiasm can be harnessed and encouraged with courses and exhibitions throughout the country, even with diplomas in botanical illustrations from some universities as well as from botanical gardens. The result is that there are simply more good illustrators in the United Kingdom than anywhere else in the world. Some are scientifically trained; others come from art schools or textile designing, or are reviving their careers after a period as mothers and housewives.

This leads me to the question: why do so many more

women than men work as botanical artists? The ratio is approximately 7:2 in my collection, a proportion that probably reflects the field as a whole. Many of the women have had careers in other areas and have switched to plant illustration after bringing up their families. In general their careers, far more than those of men, are dictated by expediency and it is hard to make a living as a botanical artist where long hours of meticulous work do not necessarily result in a fat fee.

Building up this collection has given me enormous pleasure. I have had all sorts of adventures tracking down painters, meeting them, seeing how they work and, above all, making friends with so many of them. I know there must be more wonderful artists yet to be discovered: perhaps this book will lead me to them.

In 1995 the Victoria & Albert Museum in London put on an exhibition called 'Picturing Plants', featuring paintings and prints from its own collection with an excellent catalogue by Gill Saunders. Only two contemporary paintings were included – all that the museum possesses. When the show opened John Russell Taylor wrote in *The Times*: 'The story peters out in the first half of the twentieth century … It sometimes seems there is a certain lack of confidence, perhaps concerning the continuing usefulness of botanical illustration in an age of computers.'

I am sure that anyone looking through my collection will realize that there are dozens and dozens of excellent, confident botanical artists working in the world today. It is far from true that the story 'peters out', as I hope this book will prove.

THE ARTISTS

Fay Anderson
S. Africa 16

Francesca Anderson
USA 18, 217

Gillian Barlow
UK 20, 217

Jeni Barlow
UK 217

Helen Batten
UK 24, 218

Leslie Carol Berge
USA 218

Elizabeth Blackadder
UK 26

Marjorie Blamey
UK 218

Susannah Blaxill
Australia 28, 219

Raymond C. Booth
UK 32

Jenny Brasier
UK 36, 219

Andrew Peter Brown
UK 40

Jean-Claude Victor Buytaert
Belgium 42

Elizabeth Cameron
UK 219

Richard P. Carroll
USA 44

Patricia de Chair
UK 220

Gillian Condy
S. Africa 220

Jill Coombs
UK 220

Alison Cooper
UK 46

Patricia Dale
UK 221

Pauline M. Dean
UK 48, 221

Etienne Demonte
Brazil 50, 221

Ludmyla Demonte
Brazil 221

Rosália Demonte
Brazil 52, 221

Yvonne Demonte
Brazil 54

Jakob Demus
Austria 56

Anne Ophelia Todd Dowden
USA 58

Brigid Edwards
UK 60, 222

Margaret Farr
USA 222

Ann Farrer
UK 66, 223

Jinyong Feng
China 70, 224

Ann Fraser
UK 74

Linda Funk
USA 76

Yoshio Futakuchi
Japan 78

Lawrence Greenwood
UK 80

Mary A. Grierson
UK 82, 225

Gillian Griffiths
UK 84

Noel Grunwaldt
USA 225

Coral Guest
UK 86, 225

Josephine Hague
UK 90, 226

Christine Hart-Davies
UK 94, 226

Helen Haywood
UK 96, 226

Sue Herbert
UK 98

Helga Hislop
UK 226

Jeanne Holgate
UK 100

Nicole Hornby
UK 227

Mariko Imai
Japan 102

J.P. Irani
India 227

Marilyn Jones
UK 228

Paul Jones
Australia 104

Annette de Jonquières
Denmark 108, 228

Jenny Jowett
UK 228

Yoko Kakuta
Japan 228

Sally Keir
UK 110

Martha G. Kemp
USA 229

Patricia Kessler
USA 229

Sharon Morris Kincheloe
USA 229

Christabel King
UK 112, 229

Charlotte Knox
UK 114

Mariko Kojima
Japan 116, 229

Viet Martin Kunz
Germany 118, 230

Joanna Asquith Langhorne
UK 120, 230

Katie Lee
USA 122, 230

Thalia Lincoln
S. Africa 126

Petr Liška
Czech Republic 128, 230

Elizabeth Jane Lloyd
UK 230

Rory McEwen
UK 130

Katherine Manisco
USA 134, 231

Alister Mathews
UK 231

John Morgan Matyas
USA 136

Margaret Mee
Brazil 138, 232

Lindsay Megarrity
Italy 144

Mitsuharu Mishima
Japan 146

Kate Nessler
USA 148, 232

Miyoko Okakura
Japan 150

George Olson
USA 232

Luca Palermo
Italy 152

Ronaldo Luis Pangella
Brazil 233

Jenny Phillips
Australia 154, 233

Kathy Pickles
UK 233

Marilena Pistoia
Italy 156

Jaggu Prasad
India 158

Reinhild Raistrick
UK 233

Kay Rees-Davies
UK 234

Celia Rosser
Australia 160

Graham Rust
UK 164, 234

Rosanne Sanders
UK 166

Margaret A. Saul
Australia 168, 234

Sara Anne Schofield
UK 234

Gillian Scott
Australia 170

Jenevora Searight
Brazil 235

Pandora Sellars
UK 172, 235

Vijay Kumar Sharma
India 178

Siriol Sherlock
UK 180, 235

Sheila Siegerman
Canada 186

Annika Silander-Hökerberg
Sweden 188

Alan Singer
and Arthur Singer
USA 190

Pamela Stagg
Canada 192, 235

Penny Stenning
UK 235

Margaret Stones
UK 196

Ann Swan
UK 236

Kazuto Takahashi
Japan 236

Mary Tarraway
UK 236

Jessica Tcherepnine
USA 198, 236

Michiko Toyota
Japan 200

Yoko Uchijo
Japan 202, 237

Arundhati Vartak
India 204

Alexander Viazmensky
Russia 206

Ellaphie Ward-Hilhorst
S. Africa 208

Carol Woodin
USA 237

Eleanor B. Wunderlich
USA 237

Tai-Li Zhang
China 212, 237

FAY ANDERSON

Fay Anderson was educated in India and England and is now a British citizen with permanent residence in South Africa. She received a Diploma of Fine Arts from the Michaelis School of Art, Cape Town, in 1955 and still lives in Kenilworth in Cape Town. She travelled widely in Europe, Africa, Asia and Australia but has almost exclusively concentrated on plants growing in southern Africa for her subjects.

She has completed a wealth of paintings, with many hundreds of plant studies, and has regularly published in numerous books and journals since 1967. Her latest books are *The Moraeas of southern Africa*, *The genus Watsonia* and *The woody Iridaceae* published with Kirstenbosch and the Missouri Botanical Gardens. She was awarded the RHS Grenfell Gold Medal twice and the South African Botanical Society Cythna Letty Award for botanical illustration in 1988.

She has shown widely throughout South Africa, including at the Everard Read Gallery in Johannesburg which has encouraged so many wildlife artists. Her work is in numerous botanical collections such as the Hunt Institute and The Missouri Botanical Gardens and at Kirstenbosch and Pretoria.

When I first met her in the Cape she told me that three of her best paintings were at Kew, having been selected for possible inclusion in the new edition of *The art of botanical illustration* by Wilfrid Blunt and William T. Stearn. When I returned to London I managed to track them down in the Herbarium. Two had been included in the book, although I was sadly disappointed by their colour reproduction (plates 115 & 116). The third, a pale pink amaryllis, had beautifully painted fruits, glowing like the most precious pink pearls, and immediately became my first choice. Since then I have seen a good print of it, slightly larger than life. South African prints are often excellent, with very good colour reproduction.

JERSEY LILY:
*AMARYLLIS
BELLADONNA*

Signed Fay Anderson (undated)

Acquired from the artist 1994

Watercolour on paper 470 x 320 mm

Fay Anderson

FRANCESCA ANDERSON

BORN WASHINGTON DC, USA 1946

I saw Francesca Anderson's strong, powerful black and white globe cabbage as soon as I walked through the door on my very first visit to the Hunt Institute. It was hanging in their 7th International Exhibition in 1992 and I was immediately attracted by its vitality and workmanship. I made contact with the artist shortly afterwards in Brooklyn, New York, using the invaluable Hunt Catalogue which lists artists' addresses.

She showed me a number of bold pen-and-ink drawings swirling across large sheets of paper. Despite their strength they are finely executed. She draws life-size but often chooses substantial subjects. That day I saw a splendid orchid and a number of amaryllis studies. She let me see a set of plates she was preparing to illustrate a book with M. Balick, *The palms of Belize and their uses* (still in preparation), which demonstrated that she could do the traditional identification drawings, part of the botanical illustrator's trade. She had recently completed a course for a Certificate in Botanical Illustration at the New York Botanical Gardens.

She had had a series of six solo shows in New York at Gallery 91 in the early 1970s and took a Master of Arts degree at Hunter College and a Master of Fine Arts degree in drawing and painting at Brooklyn College in 1987. After her children left home she went back to painting with a vengeance, producing work for over a dozen solo exhibitions between 1990 and 1995. One set of studies of poisonous plants was shown in a number of venues. I have a cyclamen from this series, which Francesca feels is almost spitting venom.

She took me on a number of trips to look at her work on show at the charming gallery at Wave Hill, New York, and in the Brooklyn Botanic Garden. She has just done a striking series on the venerable bonsai trees kept in the Brooklyn Garden's conservatories, beautifully observed, elegantly drawn and always with that feeling of life which permeates all her work.

She was awarded a gold medal at the RHS in 1995 for eight drawings of amaryllis, one of her favourite subjects. Sadly I did not see them as I was away at the time.

I would like far more of her drawings (I have six at the moment) but my 'wall-space-crisis' dominates my collector's passion. I need a huge space to do justice to her invigorating work. These are drawings which need to be seen life-size, and it is difficult to reproduce them in a smaller format and retain their impact.

KALE SPIRAL

Signed Francesca Anderson 4/92

Acquired from the artist 1993

Pen and ink 580 x 730 mm

CYCLAMEN

Signed Francesca Anderson
12/92

Poison Plant Series Cyclamen

Acquired from the artist 1993

Pen and ink 730 x 580 mm

GILLIAN BARLOW

BORN KHARTOUM, SUDAN 1944

Gillian Barlow trained in London at the Slade School of Fine Art, and took her Bachelor of Arts and Master of Arts degrees at the University of Sussex in the history of art, studying with Professor Quentin Bell and Dr Hans Hess.

She has held very British appointments as Herald Painter at the College of Arms in London since 1988 and as Orchid Painter for the RHS from 1995. She has had a number of one-person shows in London and New York, and in India in Bombay, Calcutta and Ahmadabad. Her most recent, highly successful, exhibition was at Spink, London, in 1995, where she showed several new works on vellum. She has illustrated a large number of books and calendars with attractive and accessible paintings.

I first saw her work at the Hunt Institute's 7th International Exhibition, where she exhibited a delicate *Gloriosa superba*. I asked her to show me some of her work in 1992 and chose a pair of extravagant yellow tulips and a classic study of an iris both in flower and with scarlet berries. The styles were very different and she told me that she had never painted anything like the tulips before, but the pair have proved great favourites when viewed in my collection.

More recently I bought a superb *Anemone hupehensis* from a show at the RHS where she received a gold medal. I particularly liked the way she handled the white flowers, such a challenge in watercolour. It is interesting to compare it with Coral Guest's painting of white lilies. Neither artist uses white, but they delineate with subtle washes of silvery grey, with pink or greenish overtones.

Another purchase has been a strong study of the kingcup *Caltha palustris*, which was awarded a Certificate of Botanical Merit at the Society of Botanical Artists. Gillian Barlow wrote to me that she was particularly pleased that I had bought these last two paintings as she felt them to be among her best.

STINKING IRIS:
IRIS FOETIDISSIMA

Signed G. Barlow 1991

Acquired from the artist 1992

Watercolour on paper 415 x 265 mm

C.BARLOW 1991

PAIR OF YELLOW PARROT TULIPS

Signed G. Barlow 1991

Acquired from the artist 1992

Watercolour on paper 260 x 365 mm

ANEMONE HUPEHENSIS

Signed G. Barlow 1994 Anemone hupehensis

Acquired from the artist 1995

Watercolour on paper 570 x 385 mm

G. Barlow '94   Anemone hupehensis

HELEN BATTEN

BORN ENGLAND 1961

Helen Batten has been a most successful freelance jewellery designer since 1984 but has recently turned her attention to watercolour paintings. She executed a large commission for 18 paintings of flowers and sea shells during 1992 and 1993 and has recently exhibited at the RHS and the Society of Botanical Artists, where she received the St Cuthbert's Mill Award and Certificate of Botanical Merit.

She trained at Bower Ashton College of Art, Bristol, and the Central School of Art and Design, London, and now has her studio in Notting Hill Gate, London.

I liked one of the group of orchids she showed at the RHS and when she delivered it she told me she was thinking of concentrating more on flower painting. I saw her work again in 1994 at the Society of Botanical Artists' show in Westminster in London and bought 'Anemone and Feathers', which I preferred to her award-winning orchid painting. She has a delicate touch.

ANEMONE AND FEATHERS

Signed Helen Batten 94

Acquired from the SBA, London 1994

Pencil and watercolour on paper 350 x 290 mm

ELIZABETH BLACKADDER

BORN FALKIRK, SCOTLAND 1931

Elizabeth Blackadder RA is a most distinguished painter whose subjects range far from the classical flower study. I love the way she places her cats among her orchids in just the same way that my two Persians roam in my conservatory, nudging aside some precious plant to make themselves comfortable.

She studied at Edinburgh University and Edinburgh College of Art and was decorated with an OBE in 1982. She has had over 40 one-person exhibitions and has work in a huge number of collections, ranging from Scotland to the United States, with paintings in the National Portrait Gallery, London, and the National Museum of Women in the Arts in Washington DC. She designed a lovely series of postage stamps of her cats in 1995 and her paintings are always immediately sold at the Royal Academy Summer Exhibition.

Her flower paintings are wonderfully free and uninhibited, yet most carefully observed. Her watercolours are splashed with spots of paint and stray pencil marks, her vigorous approach far removed from the meticulous style of the traditional botanical painter. Indeed, she

herself wrote in a foreword for an etching portfolio catalogue recently, 'I chose the plants which appealed to me as an artist and which I found visually exciting in terms of shape, colour and structure. I make no claims to botanical truth and accuracy.'

Despite this statement her plant portraits have a great feel for the character and personality of the specimen, particularly well shown in *Favourite flowers*, studies selected by Deborah Kellaway in an attractive book published by Pavilion in 1994.

Despite her 'loose and wet' technique, her plants are always immediately identifiable – indeed botanists are often astonished when they make this discovery. Her command of watercolour is quite superb, especially when painting velvety dark iris, mysterious, speckly orchids and stately lilies. It is interesting to compare her work with a Chinese brush painting of iris by Professor Jinyong Feng who has taught most of today's Chinese botanical painters in the classical mode, but who also paints with the freedom and flow of Chinese brush style.

LILIES

Signed Elizabeth Blackadder 1989

Acquired from Montpelier Studio, London 1993

Watercolour on paper 600 x 570 mm

SUSANNAH BLAXILL

BORN ARMIDALE, NEW SOUTH WALES, AUSTRALIA 1954

Susannah Blaxill is an Australian painter whose work I first saw on exhibition at David Ker's gallery in London in 1991, when she was living in England. She began painting full-time in 1985 after studying for five years at the University of East Anglia in Norwich, England. She is a very detailed and meticulous artist whose flowers, fruit and vegetables seem to float in space. She applies layer upon layer of watercolour, using very fine brushes, and achieves an almost startling intensity, clear-edged and dramatic. A beautiful painting of pears, is reproduced on the cover of the catalogue for the Hunt Institute's 7th International Exhibition (1992).

She is now back in Australia and sent work from there for a sell-out show at Spink, London, in December 1994, where it was encouraging to see paintings being snapped up with such enthusiasm. It was at this exhibition that she showed a few illustrations done on black, rather than the usual white, paper.

I have four of her paintings, two from each London show. One, a superb study of pomegranates, I have given to my son Simon who has just started his own collection of botanical paintings.

I believe she is one of today's best botanical artists and an example of Australia's depth of quality in this field.

BEETROOT

Artist's stamp SB (undated)

Acquired from Spink, London 1994

Watercolour on paper 480 x 640 mm

PANSIES

Signed Susannah Blaxill (undated)

Acquired from David Ker Gallery, London 1991

Watercolour on paper 290 x 360 mm

POMEGRANATES

Artist's stamp SB (undated)

Acquired from Spink, London 1994

Watercolour on paper 250 x 225 mm

RAYMOND C. BOOTH

BORN LEEDS, ENGLAND 1929

Raymond Booth describes himself as a painter-plantsman, and is famous for cultivating rare and difficult species and later painting them with a particularly knowledgeable eye. He trained at Leeds College of Art in the late 1940s, gaining an art teacher's diploma in 1951 after an interruption for National Service. He often uses oil on board creating strong images that reproduce well as book illustrations. He painted some lush and beautiful plates in Urquhart's *The camellia* in 1956 and 1962 (with Paul Jones) and grew most of the plants used to illustrate his recently published book *Japonica magnifica* which has text by Don Elick. Rather astonishingly, he he has neither been to Japan, nor met Elick, who lives there. The original paintings have been shown widely in the United Kingdom and the United States since the book was launched in 1992.

His first major exhibition at the Fine Art Society, London, in 1975 was mainly of wildlife, while another one in 1991 was divided into paintings of rather idealized glossy garden flowers or splendid detailed studies of individual plants. The most striking was an extraordinary study of potatoes reminiscent of a school-room poster.

His work is held in a number of public collections including the Hunt Institute, the Ulster Museum, Belfast, the Fitzwilliam Museum, Cambridge, and the RHS.

My first introduction to Raymond Booth's original work was standing on a chilly pavement outside the Fine Art Society, New Bond Street, London, queuing to get in at 7.30 in the morning. I could hardly believe that I was sixteenth in line, but I managed to buy this fine study of the red rose, *Rosa moyesii*. It appealed to me far more than the beautifully executed paintings of glossy birds amidst perfect flowers that made up a large part of the exhibition.

Finding good rose paintings seems curiously difficult today. Perhaps artists are inhibited by the perfection of all those Redouté prints. Here Raymond Booth balances scarlet rose petals with equally vibrant hips, subtly linking the two branches with a tracery of leaves and perfectly registering the changes of the seasons.

Raymond Booth grew *Tricyrtis macranthopsis* in Yorkshire and used it for a study of one of his illustrations in *Japonica magnifica*. It is normally found on the cliffs of the Kumano gorges of southern Kii, Japan, hanging from vertical, shaded ravines, often splashed with the spray of

ROSA MOYESII

Signed R.C. Booth 1988

Acquired from Fine Art Society Gallery, London 1991

Oil on paper 610 x 430 mm

waterfalls. It flowers in October, trailing waxy, bell-shaped blossoms and is found around the base of the Nachi waterfalls (a famous destination for Shinto pilgrims). The genus *Tricyrtis* (in the lily family) is made up of a dozen species most of which bear erect flowers covered in spots – the reason why they are generally called toad lilies. *T. macranthopsis* is unusual in having blossoms which hang on trailing stems. The painting shown here seems to be the same plant as that illustrated in *Japonica magnifica*, probably a study of an earlier stage of flowering. I find it more appealing than the plate in the book which, although informative, has a cluttered background.

Raymond Booth lives very quietly in Yorkshire, working in a small suburban garden crammed with greenhouses. He sometimes gardens at night with a spotlight, saving the precious daylight hours for painting. He is a very highly considered painter of flowers.

I personally prefer his more austere, academic studies, but he has a large following for both those and his more glossy, polished paintings.

TRICYRTIS MACRANTHOPSIS

Signed R.C. Booth (undated)

Acquired from Fine Art Society Gallery, London 1992

Oil on paper 450 x 325 mm

JENNY BRASIER

BORN ALVECHURCH, ENGLAND 1936

Like many other botanical artists today, Jenny Brasier had no formal training and only started painting seriously some 16 years ago. She was encouraged to do so by the late Wilfrid Blunt whose *The art of botanical illustration*, written with William T. Stearn, was first published in 1950. Her work appears in the new edition, 1994. Another source of influence and constructive criticism was John Whitehead, who has explored for plants worldwide.

She has been awarded four gold medals in RHS exhibitions and was one of the only two contemporary painters hung in 'Picturing Plants', a Victoria & Albert Museum exhibition in 1995. She has shown in the Smithsonian Institution in Washington, the Hunt Institute and has been collected by the RHS, the British Natural History Museum and many private individuals. Her work has been reproduced in a number of books on botanical painting and she provided illustrations for *Hosta: the flowering foliage plant* by Diana Grenfell (1990).

I first saw her work at the Kew Gardens Gallery in 1991. I was most impressed by her versatility and bought two widely differing works which were far removed from her more characteristic small, precise and detailed studies of fruit or cyclamen on vellum.

One is a strong and free study of a stem of bananas, done in watercolour and ink, the other a very subtle and elegant study of three *Crinum* lily flowers, predominantly executed in pencil with the most discreet monotone colouring of pink.

Later I bought a number of her small, brilliant, jewel-like watercolours on vellum, executed with meticulous and loving care. She was given several sheets of vellum that had belonged to Rory McEwen, after his death. Initially she was so intimidated she put them aside for several years, but now she works with great skill on this surface. Jenny Brasier's work is very beautiful with some of her studies having the intense quality of a medieval illuminated manuscript.

BANANAS

Signed JMB 1991

Acquired from Kew Gardens Gallery 1991

Watercolour on paper 600 x 470 mm

CYCLAMEN PURPURASCENS

Signed JMB 1994 Cyclamen purpurescens [sic] 3 forms

Acquired from the artist 1993

Watercolour on vellum 90 x 125 mm

CYCLAMEN PSEUDIBERICUM

Signed JMB 1993 Cyclamen pseudibericum 3 forms

Acquired from the artist 1994

Watercolour on vellum 90 x 125 mm

ANDREW PETER BROWN

BORN CARSHALTON, ENGLAND 1948

Dr Andrew Brown has been head of the Biology Department of Westminster School, London, since 1977. He read botany at Oxford for his BA (Hons) and completed a Ph.D. at Cambridge on 'The Vegetative History of S.W. England' in 1972.

He has always painted, although he only started to concentrate on plants relatively recently. He has had one-man shows at the Linnean Society in London and Wolfson College, Oxford, and in 1995 he was part of major exhibitions at the Hunt Institute and in the Kew Gardens Gallery. He has been awarded two gold medals and two silver gilt medals by the RHS.

Having seen a number of his precise and meticulous iris studies I commissioned him to complete an unfinished voodoo lily that he had started in 1989. This large and somewhat threatening arum lily is found in the forests of the Himalaya and South India and has the advantage that it can be grown indoors and every stage of growth recorded. Unfortunately several bulbs died while he was painting them and so it took a number of years to complete the work. These natural disasters are extremely common when painting live material. This large, complex academic study holds together remarkably well as a picture and I find it extremely satisfying.

VOODOO LILY:
SAUROMATUM VENOSUM

Signed Andrew Brown 12 August 1994

Himalaya & S. India Forests

Acquired from the artist 1994

Pencil and watercolour on paper 680 x 450 mm

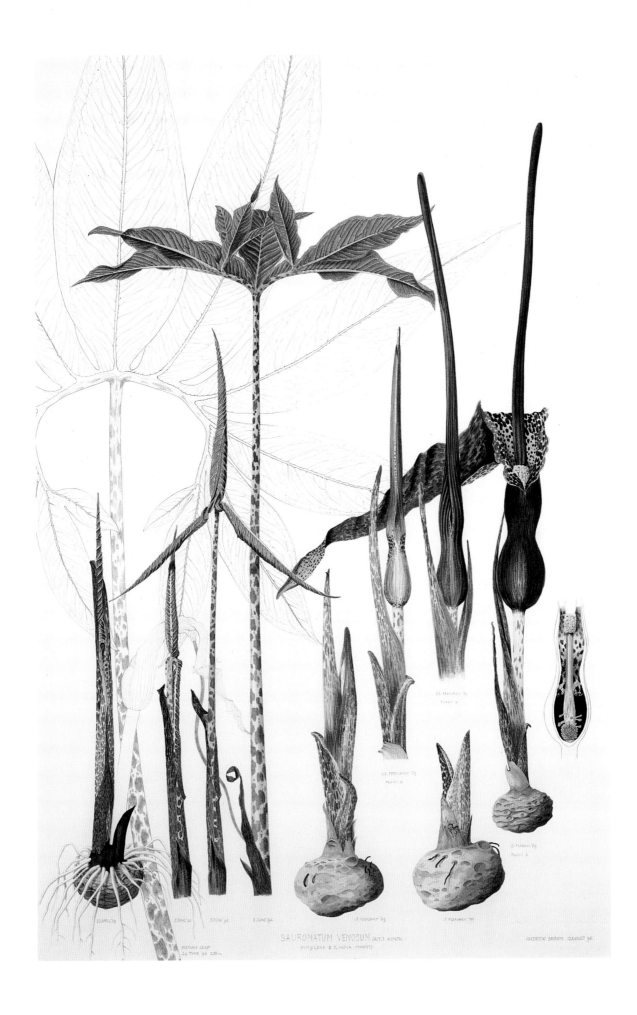

SAUROMATUM VENOSUM (AIT.) KUNTH.
HIMALAYA & N. INDIA FORESTS

ANDREW BROWN. 12 AUGUST 94.

JEAN-CLAUDE VICTOR BUYTAERT

BORN ZWARTBERG, BELGIUM 1944

A master of dry-point botanical etching, Jan Buytaert is currently a full-time sculptor, painter and graphic artist living in Antwerp who informed me his most recent theme is 'Almost Nude'. He has been professor of both botanical and drawing and graphic arts and has had one-man shows in Antwerp, in the Arboretum, Kalmthout, and at the Russian Artists' Association in St Petersburg in 1995. He has been commissioned by Queen Paola of Belgium and shown at the Hunt Institute.

He has won a number of prizes locally and is represented in the Frick Art Museum in Pittsburgh, among many other collections.

I first saw his dry-point etching of *Tolmiea menziesii* at the Hunt's 7th International Exhibition in 1992. When I wrote to him he told me there was another etching in the same series in the RHS restaurant in Vincent Square, London. Persistent enquiries ran it to earth in a cupboard with several more of his etchings. I particularly liked the *Tolmiea* I had seen at the Hunt, as I have grown this strange plant and have always been intrigued with the way new leaves spring from mature ones.

PICKABACK PLANT: *TOLMIEA MENZIESII*

Signed Jan Buytaert 1986

Acquired from the artist 1992

Dry-point etching 495 x 645 mm

RICHARD P. CARROLL

BORN SPRINGFIELD, MASSACHUSETTS, USA 1931

Here is an artist painting with incredible photo-realism whose sense of design is unfailingly strong. Richard Carroll studied painting and illustration at Syracuse University in the early 1950s and then worked for Young & Rubicam in New York and Detroit as art director and television producer. He left the advertising giant in 1974 after 20 years and worked free-lance, becoming a 'fine' artist in 1987. He has had one-man exhibitions in the Alexander F. Milliken Gallery, New York, in 1989 and in the Hokin/Kaufman Gallery, Chicago, in 1990 and was in the Hunt Institute's 7th International Exhibition in 1992.

He often works with egg tempera and achieves an extraordinary degree of detailed perfection, an artist whose painting 'Almost like Spinach', must almost be examined with a magnifying glass, before one stands back to admire it as a whole with its deliberate and satisfying juxtaposition of bark and dried leaf.

'ALMOST LIKE SPINACH'

Signed Richard Carroll 1990

Acquired from the artist 1992

Egg tempera 240 x 180 mm

© RICHARD CARROLL 1990

ALISON COOPER

BORN BENGHAZI, LIBYA 1951

Alison Cooper is the daughter of an army officer who was also a talented artist and sculptor. She studied at Newport College of Art and Florence University. She has exhibited in London at the RHS and the Society of Botanical Artists, and in Oxford and Birmingham. She lives in Worcestershire and plants from her own garden are the inspiration for her paintings.

I liked this delicate, fragile study of hardy geraniums when I saw it in a group show at the Malcolm Innes Gallery in London at the time of the Chelsea Flower Show in 1993.

HARDY GERANIUMS

Signed Alison Cooper June 91 *G. phaeum,*

Geranium ibericum, a seedling from Richard Webb

Acquired from Malcolm Innes Gallery, London 1993

Watercolour on paper 450 x 370 mm

G. phaeum

Geranium ibericum

a seedling from
Richard Webb

Alison Cooper
June. 91

PAULINE M. DEAN

BORN BRIGHTON, ENGLAND 1943

Pauline Dean was a registered nurse through the 1960s and had no formal training as a botanical artist. She started exhibiting her meticulous work in 1987 and since then she has been awarded five gold medals by the RHS, shown at the Linnean Society in London, the Hunt Institute, the Everard Read Gallery, Johannesburg, and illustrated a number of books. The horticultural journal *The New Plantsman* has commissioned her to paint a number of plants, most of which grow at the RHS Garden at Wisley in Surrey, only a few miles from where she now lives.

She is the tutor on the botanical art courses which have been run by the RHS at Wisley since 1994, and designed the successful series of 'Winter Flower' plates for the RHS and Royal Worcester.

I bought a watercolour of a horse chestnut from her show at Kew Gardens Gallery in 1991. She has perfectly captured the way the conkers glow in polished splendour.

Later I acquired a precise and immaculate academic study of that showy toadstool the fly agaric, with its warning scarlet cap splashed with white spots. She shows every stage to perfection with pristine clarity. It is interesting to compare it with the same subject by 'Sasha' Viazmensky later in this volume.

FLY AGARIC: *AMANITA MUSCARIA*

Signed P.M. Dean (undated)

Acquired from the RHS Show 1993

Watercolour on paper 290 x 435 mm

ETIENNE DEMONTE

BORN NITERÓI, BRAZIL 1931

Etienne Demonte is one of an almost legendary family of plant and animal painters who live way up in the mountains above Rio de Janeiro, in Petrópolis. His childhood was spent in Niterói where he and his sisters, Rosália and Yvonne, were taken into the surrounding forests and along the Atlantic coast by their father. They all started painting at an early age. Etienne now has two grown-up sons of his own, André and Rodrigo, who also paint wildlife. They are all passionate conservationists and spend a lot of their time on field trips with scientists and ecologists, taking notes, sketches and photographs to be worked on in their studios. Although the Amazon is the most publicized area under threat in Brazil, there are others such as the Atlantic rainforest and the north-eastern desert where the wildlife is probably under even greater stress and they have worked there too.

Etienne Demonte is an attractive, gentle artist who paints birds quite beautifully. He had no formal training but has developed a detailed, meticulous and sometimes ornate style. He is particularly well known for his paintings of humming-birds.

He has had over half a dozen exhibitions in the United States, England and Spain and over 20 shows in Brazil. He has won prizes for his postage stamp designs and produced a number of portfolios on birds. He has done a lot of broadcasting and television in which he emphasizes conservation and his concerns about the environment.

I saw his work first in a booklet called *For Love of Nature*, compiled by James White, and then later at the Hunt Institute. When I met him I chose a study for the directness and skill with which he had painted an ornamental banana tree which grew just outside his house. The flower was being pollinated by a vivid humming-bird taking the nectar. Later I commissioned him to paint me a striking bauhinia, a beautiful flowering tree which grew in his garden, again with a humming-bird pollinator. He lives at the end of a challenging track in a house surrounded by trees, in the cooler climate near Petrópolis.

The Demonte family has developed its own style of painting among themselves. I prefer their simpler watercolours and gouache works, but they do some highly elaborate paintings in oil as well, which seem to be much favoured in South America.

ORNAMENTAL BANANA: *MUSA VELUTINA*

Planalto Hermit Humming-bird: *Phaethornis pretrei*

Signed Etienne Demonte 1993

Acquired from the artist 1994

Gouache on paper 700 x 480 mm

ROSALIA DEMONTE

BORN NITERÓI, BRAZIL 1932

osália Demonte lives in Petrópolis, the high altitude town in the mountains behind Rio where the *carioca* retreat when the weather gets too hot and humid in the city. She and her sister, Yvonne, share a studio next to their house with Ludmyla, one of Rosália's daughters. Rosália's brother, Etienne Demonte, lives nearby where he paints alongside his two sons. None of them has had any extensive formal training and their styles of painting are sometimes very similar. Rosália tends to concentrate on flowers and butterflies, while her daughter paints dramatic pictures of the wild cats of South America.

I first heard about the family through *Flora and fauna of Brazil*, a mixture of essays and plates showing a range of their work. The book was written by Chrystiane Ferraz Blower, another of Rosália's daughters, so keeping it in the family yet again.

I was driven to Petrópolis on what can only be described as a terrifying road. It passes through quite magnificent scenery, with great vistas of Atlantic rainforest stretching down the mountainside, but the narrow winding road overlooks precipitous falls and areas where torrential streams have swept away the protective parapets. Just as we reached the Demontes' house the front wheel came off the car and I can only be thankful it did not happen earlier, on one of the hairpin curves on the road up from Rio.

To study their subjects in the wild, Rosália, Yvonne and Ludmyla take off into the jungle in a big camper driven by Richard Blower, Rosália's husband. They use it as a base for several weeks, asking the local people to bring them specimens to paint. It was on one of these trips near the town of Caitité in Bahia that Rosália found the rare *Langsdorffia hypogea*, a curious root-parasite of the family Balanophoraceae. She painted this subject for me from her notes using a large sheet of vellum that had originally belonged to Rory McEwen, which she was given by the Hunt Institute. Later I realized that she had also painted another version, for the Hunt's collection.

She has exhibited in London, Madrid and New York, as well as being part of a large show at the Hunt, with an emphasis on Brazilian ecology.

Another painting of hers is an extraordinary vine, *Aristolochia gigantea*, which grows up a steep bank in her garden. The specimen she painted for this dramatic picture, with its striking maroon and white flower, was given to her by Roberto Burle Marx, the famous landscape designer who was such a great friend of Margaret Mee.

LANGSDORFFIA HYPOGEA

Signed R. Demmonte [sic] (undated)

Acquired from the artist 1992

Gouache on vellum (from the estate of Rory McEwen,
supplied by the Hunt Institute) 550 x 410 mm

YVONNE DEMONTE

BORN NITERÓI, BRAZIL 1932

Although Yvonne Demonte studied at the School of Fine Arts, Rio de Janeiro, it was only for a very brief period and she feels that the real stimulus for her talent was the work of wildlife painters such as Audubon, Roger Tory Peterson and Arthur Singer whom she studied later.

She has spent much time in Brazil's wilder places such as the Itatiaia National Park, around the river Amambai in Mato Grosso do Sul, in the backlands of Bahia and in the Pantanal. Generally she goes with her sister Rosália on expeditions organized by Rosália's husband.

She worked with the naturalist Augusto Ruschi, illustrating all the pen-and-ink reproductions in one of the volumes of *Birds of Brazil* (*Aves do Brasil*), has been commissioned for two sets of postage stamps and illustrated encyclopedias and scientific books. But the books of hers I remember best were for children. Each one was about a particular animal and its environment, showing where it lived, what it ate and what its babies looked like, the whole book being shaped to the outline of the sloth, tamarin monkey or jaguar that she was describing. They were designed to encourage children to become environmentally conscious in the most appealing way and typified all the Demontes' passionate involvement with Brazil's endangered wildlife.

I saw this bromeliad on the very first visit I made to Rosália and Yvonne's studio in Petrópolis. It was unfinished but I liked its subtle, quiet tones and asked her to complete it for me. She had found it growing in the Atlantic rainforest near Petrópolis.

BROMELIAD

Signed Yvonne Demonte 1992

Commissioned 1992

Gouache on paper 690 x 490 mm

Yvonne Lemaitre
1992

JAKOB DEMUS

BORN VIENNA, AUSTRIA 1959

Jakob Demus trained as a sculptor at the Vienna Academy where he studied sculpture, anatomy and drawing in master classes under Joannis Avramidis. His passionate love for nature eventually made him decide to concentrate on painting and the graphic arts.

He is an artist who is much influenced by the past. He has not only studied the work of Pieter Breughel the Elder, Claude and the Dutch painters of the seventeenth century, but he also uses their techniques, grinding and mixing his own colours and making extracts of wood smoke to create the warm tones of his bistre.

As well as flowers Demus also draws intensely detailed studies of rocks and stones and delicate landscapes. His work has been exhibited widely, in Tokyo, Vienna, Munich and New York and is held in the British Museum, the Victoria & Albert in London, the Metropolitan Museum of Art, New York, the Rijksmuseum, Amsterdam, and many other centres.

When I first saw his diamond-needle dry-point etching of a thistle at the Hunt Institute's 7th International Exhibition in 1992 I felt it was the best drawing of a thistle I had ever seen. Sadly it was not available, but later I saw a whole range of his flower etchings and chose this beautiful ranunculus instead. I deliberately mounted it in an antique-style frame and it hangs in a panelled room in our old house. It is one of the drawings I treasure most.

RANUNCULUS ASIATICUS

Signed Jakob Demus 1988 7/30 II et

Acquired from G.C. Boerner Gallery, New York 1992

Diamond-needle dry-point etching 260 x 210 mm

7/30 II.ét.   Jakob Semey.   1988.

ANNE OPHELIA TODD DOWDEN

BORN DENVER, COLORADO, USA 1907

Like many other botanical artists, Anne Ophelia Dowden started off earning her way as a textile designer and teacher, only later following her early interest in plants. By the time she had trained at Boulder and taken her BA at the Carnegie Institute of Technology and Fine Arts the Depression was gripping the United States and jobs were hard to find. Eventually she became part of a successful group, producing wallpaper and fabric designs. As head of the art department at Manhattanville College, New York, for 23 years from 1932 to 1955, she saw many young artists develop.

Although she had painted flowers all her life, it was in 1952 that she really started to establish herself as a botanical artist. Her first project was *Look at a flower*, a book for children which she wrote and illustrated and which stayed in print for 22 years. From then on she has always had a book in preparation, sometimes illustrating another writer's work, but often doing a one-woman project where she writes the text and paints the pictures. Reading through the three-page book list she sent me, it seems that her most recent is *Poisons in our path: plants that harm and heal* which she wrote and illustrated for HarperCollins in 1994 (at the age of 87).

While browsing through the Hunt Institute's collection I came across a number of her paintings. James White, the curator, told me she was still active and I traced her back to Boulder, Colorado, to which she has recently returned – she spent her childhood there. It turned out that she and my husband's mother were both on Carnegie Mellon campus at about the same time, and they shared a friend in common. Now three productive and bright octogenarians have rediscovered each other.

When she heard I wanted to add one of her paintings to my collection she responded quickly and sent me 'Squash Blossom 1978', a painting which she had had made into a print by the Frame House Gallery. She had kept it since then and I was pleased to get one of her earlier works for my collection.

SQUASH BLOSSOM 1978

Signed Anne Ophelia Dowden (undated)

Acquired from the artist 1994

Watercolour on paper 350 x 460 mm

BRIGID EDWARDS

BORN LONDON, ENGLAND 1940

Brigid Edwards has worked as a botanical illustrator for nearly ten years. After a successful career as a television producer and director she became inspired by the work of the Bauer brothers and Ehret in the eighteenth century and started to paint flowers from her lovely village garden. She is one of those rare botanical artists who have been hung recently in the Royal Academy Summer Show (1990).

I first saw her work at the Hunt Institute and, realizing that she lived near me, went to see her work. Her Royal Academy exhibit 'Magnolia Fruit and Leaves' is a small gem. As so often happens with plant painters who work very slowly, she had hardly anything to show me on my first visit in 1992. I immediately commissioned studies of a robust artichoke flower and two rusty-red onions. In 1994 she had a remarkable show at Kew Gardens Gallery where the critics compared her work with that of Rory McEwen, one of the standard-bearers of today's renaissance in botanical painting. Like McEwen she often works on vellum, painting with a glowing, quiet brilliance, sometimes framing her pictures like medieval treasures. She painted all the plates for John Richards' *Primulas* (1994). The RHS has twice awarded her a gold medal.

She had a wonderfully successful exhibition at Thomas Gibson Fine Arts Ltd in London's Old Bond Street at the end of 1995, where all her paintings were sold before the show opened.

Brigid Edwards is undoubtedly one of today's finest botanical artists asnd I am particularly attracted to her work on vellum.

ARTICHOKE FLOWER

Signed Brigid Edwards 1989

Acquired from the artist 1992

Watercolour over pencil on vellum 360 x 260 mm

CAPE GOOSEBERRY

Signed Brigid Edwards 1993

Acquired from Kew Gardens
Gallery 1994

Watercolour over pencil on
vellum 190 x 125 mm

DOUGLAS FIR: *PSEUDOTSUGA MENZIESII*

Signed Brigid Edwards 1993
Pseudotsuga menziesii x $2\frac{1}{2}$,
with acknowledgements to
Professor William Henlow

Acquired from Kew Gardens
Gallery 1994

Watercolour over pencil on
vellum 250 x 180 mm

Pseudotsuga menziesii x 2½
with acknowledgements to Professor William Stearn

Brigid Edwards 1993

REDCURRANTS

Signed Brigid Edwards 1993

Acquired from Kew Gardens
   Gallery 1994

Watercolour over pencil on
   vellum 200 x 165 mm

KOHLRABI

Signed Brigid Edwards 1993

Acquired from Kew Gardens
   Gallery 1994

Watercolour over pencil on
   vellum 445 x 303 mm

ANN FARRER

BORN MELBOURNE, AUSTRALIA 1950

Known affectionately as Annie, Ann Farrer is a familiar figure at Kew, having painted innumerable plates for *The Kew Magazine* (now, once more, called *Curtis's Botanical Magazine*), *The Plantsman* and *The New Plantsman*.

She did some particularly dramatic paintings recently for a Kew monograph *The genus Arum*.

When she is not freelancing at Kew, she is probably leading a trekking party in some remote part of the Himalaya. She recently came back from Nepal looking fit and bronzed. Perhaps she inherited this passion for far-away places from her relative, the famous botanical explorer Reginald Farrer (1880–1920) who travelled widely in China and Burma and introduced many plants into Western gardens.

She took a degree in English and history of art at Manchester. In 1977 she was awarded a Churchill travelling scholarship which took her to Kashmir and Ladakh to draw the illustrations for *Flowers of the Himalaya* with text by O. Polunin and A. Stainton (1984).

She has been awarded six gold medals by the RHS and was the first recipient of the Jill Smythies award by the Linnean Society in London in 1988. She has illustrated many books, taught some of the 'Margaret Mee Foundation' students from Brazil and now teaches an annual course in botanical illustration at Kew. Her paintings have been exhibited in the Kew Gardens Gallery, at Lancaster University and at the most recent (1995) Hunt Institute's International Exhibition.

The first work of hers I bought was a set of six watercolours which Spink, London, had made into a limited edition of prints. The subjects were plants from six different endangered rainforest areas around the world. She got her plants from Kew and painted them there. It was hard to choose one of the six to illustrate here, but eventually I chose *Begonia chlorosticta* which was first discovered in 1967 in the Hose Mountains of Sarawak. The plant's dramatically blotched and spotted leaves are brilliantly observed and the composition has depth and strength.

Later I asked Annie to paint some of my favourite plants, which involved her coming down to my home near Oxford to capture their 'feel' in my garden. She painted two of my favourite clematis, *C. orientalis* and *C.* 'Miss Bateman', and two fine trees from the garden, a swamp cypress and a cedar of Lebanon. I was particularly anxious to have her paint the cedar. Four were originally marked on a map dated about 1720. One was felled before we bought Hinton and one must have been storm-damaged years ago, leaving a rather distorted tree with cones on conveniently accessible lower branches, sweeping on to the lawn. The two other cedars are in good condition, but must be nearing the end of their lifespan. I chose Annie to paint one of them and the cypress as she is particularly good with conifers, weaving subtle patterns with their needle-shaped leaves.

It was not as simple as it might seem to execute these commissions. She started late one spring with *Clematis* 'Miss Bateman', then the next year my specimen produced uncharacteristic flowers, set back by some bad weather. Annie then bought one from a nursery but unfortunately it died. So it took three years to finish. The swamp cypress was just as difficult: having produced cones in abundance one season, it did not cone again for two years. It is a deciduous conifer and has a particularly beautiful late-autumn foliage of flaming, rusty red which turns my tree into a burning spire. I well remember driving to London with needles falling off *en route* and mostly shed before I gave the almost naked branches to Annie, so that she could complete the picture at last.

BEGONIA CHLOROSTICTA

Signed Ann Farrer 1990

Acquired from the artist 1991

Watercolour on paper 330 x 260 mm

CLEMATIS ORIENTALIS

Signed Ann Farrer 1991

Commissioned 1991

Watercolour on paper 590 x 465 mm

CEDAR OF LEBANON

Signed Ann Farrer 91/92

Commissioned 1991, received 1992

Watercolour on paper 550 x 680 mm

JINYONG FENG

BORN YIXING, JIANGSU PROVINCE, CHINA 1925

Professor Feng has all the appearance of a distinguished Chinese academic with a fresh and rosy face, white hair, twinkling eyes and a relaxed, friendly and yet dignified manner. He has taught most of the botanical illustrators in China during the course of his long career and won major prizes in his own country as well as exhibiting abroad at the Hunt Institute, the Missouri Botanical Gardens, in Sydney, in Japan and at the Everard Read Gallery in Johannesburg. He is now retired from his final position which he described as 'senior engineer' at the Botanical Institute in Beijing.

Inititally I wrote to the institute to try and make contact. After a lengthy pause it transpired that he had been away for a year, visiting his daughter in Canada. Eventually I was able to go very briefly to Beijing where I met him, his wife and several colleagues. Communication was a real problem because, although he understands some English and writes it well, we had to talk through a rather uncooperative translator. The botanical garden is on the outskirts of Beijing in a semi-agricultural area where the roads are thronged with trucks and bicycles. We walked around the gardens which were filled with people admiring the spectacular beds of peonies.

I looked through Feng's portfolio in the institute's reception room, sipping the customary tea. I found his work exceptionally fine, particularly his older pieces painted some years previously. He showed me some line drawings of great beauty, executed with a brush made of just three hairs from a wolf's tail; even under a powerful magnifying glass they were breathtaking. Thousands were done for Volumes 1–78 of the vast *Flora Reipublicae Popularis Sinicae* (1959–1989), where every plant is illustrated by a small line drawing on each flimsy page. He also had a number of watercolours, some gouache and some studies that appeared to have been done on paper with oil. (All the artists that I met in Beijing were particularly proud of their oil paintings, but I generally found them much less refined than watercolour or gouache.) I wanted to buy some of Feng's older paintings of camellias but he was very reluctant and offered to copy them for me. This is a very alien approach for a Westerner, but it is totally within the Chinese tradition. Eventually we agreed that I would buy one older painting, a small treasure of *Camellia chekiangolesa* that has already been published as a journal cover, and a recent painting of the newly discovered *Camellia chrysantha* executed on Winsor & Newton paper brought back from his visit to Canada. Feng also parted with a lyrical, less formal oil painting of a pink hibiscus, *H. syriacus*. As a charming gesture he gave me a flowing brush-painting of iris mounted on a silk surround, called 'Butterflies before the Wind', which reminded me slightly of Elizabeth Blackadder's work. At the end of our meeting I agreed, rather uncertainly, that he would copy a white *Camellia vietnamensis* for me. It is a success and almost has the quality of the original which he painted when he was younger.

CAMELLIA CHEKIANGOLESA

Signed with Chinese characters

Acquired from the artist 1994

Watercolour on paper 245 x 160 mm

浙江红花油茶 Camellia chekiangoleca Hu, sp. nov.

'BUTTERFLIES BEFORE THE WIND'

Signed with his chop, 'Butterflies before the wind' (Iris) by Jinyong Feng,
Institute of Botany, Academia Sinica, Beijing, China

Gift from the artist 1994

Watercolour on paper 660 x 480 mm

HIBISCUS SYRIACUS

Signed with his chop

Aquired from the artist 1994

Oil on paper 400 x 280 mm

ANN FRASER

BORN INDIA 1936

Lady Ann Fraser spent her early childhood in Kashmir, returning to an upbringing on the Scottish Borders. She had little formal training as a flower painter, only beginning when her four sons left home and finished using her garden as a football pitch. She and her husband, Sir Charles Fraser, started gardening seriously in 1985, converting their one-acre plot at Shepherd House, Inveresk, into an enchanting place described in Rosemary Verey's recent book *Secret gardens* (and open to the public on occasions in the summer). They filled it with a potent array of interesting flowers, planted in subtle and unusual combinations. The ever-changing borders were a powerful stimulus to Ann Fraser's painting and she set up her studio in a small conservatory attached to the seventeenth-century house.

I first saw her work in a group show at the Malcolm Innes Gallery in London in 1994, where I bought her 'The Black Border'. By then she had shown widely in Scotland and as far afield as the Everard Read Gallery in Johannesburg. All her subjects are from her own garden or conservatory. When I visited Shepherd House later in 1994 I was shown a remarkable series of 12 paintings, one for each month, of an array of seasonal border flowers. Each month's selection was skilfully designed and beautifully painted and I hope that one day they will be reproduced well enough to do justice to her 'calendar' series.

THE BLACK BORDER

Signed Ann Fraser September 93

Acquired from Malcolm Innes Gallery, London 1994

Watercolour on paper 480 x 660 mm

LINDA FUNK

BORN OAK PARK, ILLINOIS, USA 1937

Linda Funk is a highly considered teacher who runs very popular courses at Blue Hill in Maine during the summer. She has had a substantial number of solo exhibitions in venues ranging from Longwood Gardens in Pennsylvania to Ursus Prints in New York and the Atlantic Gallery in Washington DC. Recently she has been preoccupied with designing and executing 56 cabinet panels decorated with large-scale botanical oil paintings, in Northeast Harbor, Maine.

She has been a freelance designer and illustrator since 1979. Her work in botanical illustration was enhanced with a course led by Claire Roberts at Flatford Mill, Essex, England, in 1985, followed by study at Eagle Hill Wildlife Research Station, Steuben, Maine, with Biruta Hansen in 1988.

I first heard about her from a friend in New Orleans who was tremendously enthusiastic about her teaching and illustrations. She arranged for Linda to send me a number of transparencies of her latest paintings. Although I liked what I saw, I felt reluctant to make a substantial purchase without seeing the work properly, and I did not have the opportunity to visit her studio in Maine. Eventually our paths coincided in New York when Linda drove down with her car filled with paintings, stacked them on a mobile luggage rack and wheeled them through the streets of Manhattan to my hotel. She turned out to be an attractive and lively woman who I can well understand would be an inspiring teacher.

I bought a watercolour and graphite pencil study of *Zinnia elegans*. She has drawn the rusty red, pink and orange zinnia flowers to perfection and her use of pencil alone on a bud and some of the stems (a 'trade mark' of hers) makes for a very satisfying whole. The painting of the veins on the undersurface of the petals is particularly sensitive. This painting really runs the gamut between botanical illustration and artistic expression at its best.

ZINNIA ELEGANS

Signed Linda Funk 1995

Acquired from the artist 1995

Pencil and watercolour on paper 430 x 540 mm

76

YOSHIO FUTAKUCHI

BORN ISHIKAWA, JAPAN 1900

Yoshio Futakuchi is the oldest artist in my collection. He is immensely respected in Japan as an artist and a teacher and still works with younger painters like Michiko Toyota, who frequently visit his studio. I contacted him through Michiko who sent me transparencies of some of his work. I chose *Camellia sasanqua* which he executed at the age of 94. She also sent me a recent photograph of him looking composed and serious, surrounded by his work, sitting in his navy-blue painting smock in his studio where he still draws every day. There are at least ten different plant portraits around him, some really large, others detailed studies, all showing his mastery of design and lay-out.

He has illustrated half a dozen books, the latest of which is *The picture book of camellias* published in 1992. He sent me a signed copy with a dedication in beautifully executed Japanese characters. The paintings are loose and relaxed, without the precision and finesse of many contemporary artists, but they do show the form and character of each variety of camellia.

He attended the Tokyo University of Arts in 1925 and worked at the department of science, Tokyo University, for ten years from 1927. He has had many one-man and group exhibitions in the last 20 years and showed at the Hunt Institute in 1988 in its 6th International Exhibition. His paintings have appeared in a number of horticultural books published in Japan. It is wonderful that he has been having such a productive and respected old age.

CAMELLIA SASANQUA

Signed Y. Futakuchi (undated)

Acquired from the artist 1994

Watercolour, gouache on paper 325 x 235 mm

Y. Futakuchi

BORN TODMORDEN, ENGLAND 1915

Before World War II Lawrence Greenwood worked as a carpet designer, engineering draughtsman and a general manager in industry. He started painting flowers in 1968 and attended evening classes at his local art school for five years. For the last 20 years he has exhibited his work at the shows of the Alpine Garden Society and Scottish Rock Garden Club. He showed 40 paintings at each of the 5th and 6th Rock Garden Conferences held at Nottingham University in 1981 and Warwick University in 1991.

Most botanical illustrators will not paint from photographs, mainly because the camera can never show those parts of the plant which are hidden behind other parts. Illustrators need to be able to look round the back and see what is there, as well as having the live plant in front of them. Lawrence Greenwood, however, is one of those unusual painters who is able to produce a painting from a photograph provided that the latter is of high quality. Because of this skill he has been able to paint plants which are not in cultivation by using transparencies taken by botanists on their plant-hunting travels around the world. Most recently he has painted rare and inacessible species from the Himalaya, Chile and Argentina – watercolours which have amazed the botanists and gardeners who have seen them.

Lawrence produces two kinds of painting. The first is the traditional 'botanical illustration' of a plant set on a white background; the rhododendron shown here is an example. The second is of the plant set in its habitat, perhaps a woodland plant growing among fallen dead leaves or an alpine species nestling in the rocks and stones of a scree slope: the background is painted in as much careful detail as is the botanical subject of the study.

His illustration of a *Calochortus* was published in *The New Plantsman* in 1994 and further paintings will be published in future issues.

I bought one of his paintings after seeing his work at the Hunt Institute's 7th International Exhibition in 1992. I have always admired the yellow rhododendrons although to my great regret I cannot grow them in my alkaline soil. He has painted the foreshortened leaves with particular skill.

RHODODENDRON FALCONERI

Signed L.G. Rhododendron falconeri

Acquired from the artist 1992

Watercolour on paper 335 x 455 mm

Rhododendron falconeri

MARY A. GRIERSON

BORN BANGOR, NORTH WALES 1912

Mary Grierson is one of those warm, attractive women who must be everyone's favourite aunt. I met her first at Kew and then later as one of the judges on the RHS flower painting committee. The first paintings of hers that I bought were from an exhibition at Spink, London, where she has shown for many years.

She honed her observational skills as a Women's Auxiliary Air Force flight officer interpreting aerial photographs during World War II, and later worked as a cartographer. But in 1960, when she was nearing 50, she started a new career as the official botanical illustrator at Kew, encouraged by John Nash RA whom she first encountered at a series of courses on botanical painting at Flatford Mill, Essex, which she used to attend during her holidays. She remained at Kew until the early 1970s and is still to be seen at all the important shows in its gallery. She was awarded five gold medals by the RHS and received their Veitch Memorial Medal in 1984. In 1986 she received an honorary doctorate in philosophy from Reading University.

She has produced postage stamps and many designs for the Franklin Mint's commemorative china and her work is in the British Museum, the Natural History Museum, London, and at Kew. She has illustrated a plethora of books from *Mountain flowers* by Anthony Huxley in 1967 to *Hellebores* by Brian Mathew in 1989, as well as painting numerous plates for *Curtis's Botanical Magazine*. She also painted the plates for the huge *Orchidaceae* by P.F. Hunt.

She was invited to Hawaii in the 1970s and 1980s to record its native flora. Tht work will be published soon as *A Hawai'ian florilegium*.

I have never met an artist who has enjoyed her painting life more. She still always has some painting 'on the go' and gives thanks for her eyesight because she is still an active plant illustrator.

YELLOW WATER LILY

Signed Mary Grierson (undated)

Acquired from Spink, London 1990

Watercolour on paper 260 x 340 mm

THE GREAT SUNFLOWER: *HELIANTHUS ANNUUS*

Signed Mary Grierson July '92

Acquired from Kew Gardens Gallery 1993

Watercolour on paper 400 x 300 mm

Helianthus annuus
The Great sunflower
July '92 Mary Grierson.

GILLIAN GRIFFITHS

BORN BRIDGEND, WALES 1946

As a preliminary career to flower painting, Gillian Griffiths' previous life as a police secretary for 23 years is certainly unique among the artists in my collection. Botanical painting started off as a hobby and then became a full-time obsession. Since 1990 she has had several exhibitions in Wales. She was awarded a gold medal by the RHS in 1986 and two silver gilt medals later. She now teaches adults the joys of painting in watercolour.

I bought this study of *Sarracenia purpurea* ssp. *purpurea*, a North American carnivorous plant, after seeing it at an RHS show. I have always been intrigued with those rather sinister plants that supplement their diets by attracting insects into their vase-like leaves where they are trapped and ultimately digested in the fluid at the base.

SARRACENIA PURPUREA SSP. PURPUREA

Signed G. Griffiths, *Sarracenia purpurea* ssp. *purpurea* (undated)

Acquired from the RHS Show 1993

Watercolour on paper 455 x 305 mm

Sarracenia purpurea ssp. purpurea.

G. Griffiths.

CORAL GUEST

Coral Guest just beams with enthusiasm as she talks about illustrating flowers. Her studio is rather sparse, not hung with paintings, as she can always sell her work immediately it is finished. She often uses substantial pieces of paper and paints strong, large plants, life-size, suspending them in space. Occasionally she will show some tiny seedhead hovering in the centre of a huge white expanse which I find very oriental.

She was trained at the Harrow School of Art and Chelsea School of Art and later won a travel scholarship to Japan and studied Zen calligraphic painting at Seitei-Ji, Jamanashi prefecture. She painted the native flora there as well as working as a screen-painter. By 1986 she had become a freelance botanical illustrator and had started lecturing on watercolour techniques. The RHS awarded her gold medals in 1984 and 1986. She has had five one-person exhibitions in London, New York and The Hague, Holland, and is represented in several public collections including the Sechuan Academy, China. She painted at Monet's garden at Giverny, France, for *The Artist* magazine and has taught at each 'Painting Flowers' workshop at Kew since 1993.

I was sitting in a restaurant near Edinburgh, admiring some glorious flower prints. Closer examination made me realize that I was at last looking at large, original paintings by Coral Guest, who I had somehow missed seeing before. Shortly afterwards I bought a vast and splendid painting of *Paeonia* 'Sarah Bernhardt' and was so carried away with enthusiasm that I did not even consider where I was going to hang it on my crowded walls.

Later I commissioned her to paint me a white lily as she revelled in the challenge of white subjects. Eventually *Lilium longiflorum* 'Ice Queen' arrived, accompanied by some interesting comments on technique: 'Please note that however deceptive it might appear, there is most certainly no white paint on this work. All is achieved with skilled washes of varying greys and remains true to the purest traditions of watercolour.' I find the design one of the most unusual and interesting in my collection and love the subtlety of the grey-green leaves.

PAEONIA 'SARAH BERNHARDT'

Signed Coral Guest '93

Acquired from the artist 1994

Watercolour on paper 880 x 600 mm

LILIUM LONGIFLORUM 'ICE QUEEN'

Signed Coral Guest 1995

Commissioned 1995

Watercolour on paper 760 x 570 mm

JOSEPHINE HAGUE

BORN LIVERPOOL, ENGLAND 1928

Josephine Hague studied textile design at Liverpool College of Art, returning to the college years later for a refresher course. From 1979 to 1995 she followed a freelance career in textile design and illustration and her work has been exhibited in many galleries including Kew Gardens Gallery, the National Theatre in London and the Tryon Gallery, London. Her exhibits at the RHS have included a set of paintings of species and cultivars of ivy, and a series of portraits of *Sorbus* species which will be used to illustrate a forthcoming monograph on the genus by Hugh MacAllister and Nigel Taylor. Between 1984 and 1988, the RHS awarded her four gold medals and in 1993 she was invited to become artist in residence at the Liverpool Museum of Natural History. She has designed a series of British wildflower plates for The Conservation Foundation.

She lives near to Ness Gardens, the botanic garden attached to the University of Liverpool, which provides her with many of her subjects. In common with most other botanical illustrators, she only paints from life or from working drawings. Her finished paintings are both bold and accurately observed.

I have a couple of working drawings – charming studies of *Clematis* 'Vyvyan Pennell' – in the collection which demonstrate the way in which the layers of paint are built up until the correct colour is achieved.

Jo Hague would come to my country house and paint in the orangery. I asked her to do the morning glory 'Heavenly Blue', one of my favourite clematis, 'Elsa Späth', and a study of the many varieties of *Streptocarpus* that I love to grow. I remember her leaving, laden with different plants, anxious to see if she could grow them too.

PANSIES AND *TROPAEOLUM SPECIOSUM*

Signed Josephine Hague (undated)

Acquired from Kew Gardens Gallery 1990

Watercolour on paper 380 x 280 mm

Josephine Hogue

STUDIES OF *STREPTOCARPUS*

Signed Josephine Hague (undated)

Commissioned 1992

Watercolour on paper 510 x 400 mm

MORNING GLORY

Signed Josephine Hague 1990

Delivered 1991

Watercolour on paper 310 x 360 mm

CHRISTINE HART-DAVIES

BORN SHREWSBURY, ENGLAND 1947

Christine Hart-Davies is particularly well known for her miniatures of flowers, landscapes and gardens and for her detailed and precise studies of mosses and lichens. She has been awarded five gold medals by the RHS, is a founder member of the Society of Botanical Artists and was their honorary secretary for ten years. Her meticulous flower paintings illustrated Henry Bright's *A year in a Victorian garden* (1989) and she has been commissioned to paint for *The Kew Magazine*.

She contributed black-and-white drawings to *The new Royal Horticultural Society dictionary of gardening* (ed. A. Huxley).

After travelling extensively in Europe and North Africa, she settled in Dorset in 1975. She still travels to Europe, Australia and the Americas making studies of the native flora. Recently she joined an expedition to Sumatra to paint plants in the rainforest.

Although her miniatures are beautifully painted I have somehow never got very excited by any contemporary artist's work in this field. I bided my time and eventually bought two excellent life-size paintings at Kew Gardens Gallery. One shows the tiny Albany pitcher plant, *Cephalotus follicularis*, with its small, barrel-shaped leaves crowded together on a mossy bank waiting for some unwary insect to venture in. The other is perhaps rather uncharacteristic of her work: an arresting study of an Australian kangaroo paw plant, *Anigozanthus manglesii*, upon which every artist focuses when show the collection. Its scarlet, hairy stems create the most striking pattern and contrast with the green, paw-shaped flowers.

KANGAROO PAW: *ANIGOZANTHUS MANGLESII*

Signed Christine Hart-Davies (undated)

Acquired from Kew Gardens Gallery 1994

Watercolour on paper 375 x 280 mm

HELEN HAYWOOD

BORN LONDON 1964

Helen Haywood spent her childhood in Sussex, near Ashdown forest, and moved to Wales in her teens. She studied for her BA degree at Gwent, and took a Masters in illustration at Birmingham. She did some teaching and enjoyed making jewellery.

She had always had a passionate interest in nature and in conservation and won the 'Young Illustrator of the Year' award in 1988; it was presented to her by Sir David Attenborough. She has done illustrations for *The Kew Magazine* and the Reader's Digest *A garden for all seasons*.

Her most important exhibition so far was in 1994 at the Museum of Garden History in London. She showed a selection of paintings with some smaller studies on vellum: most were botanical but a few were of insects and delighted all who saw them. It was there that I bought a wild cabbage with flowers, roots and crinkly leaves as well as two small paintings on vellum. For my son Simon's collection I chose a superb thistle as his first purchase. Her leaves and thorns are particularly well observed and she deserves the growing number of enthusiasts for her work.

THISTLE

Signed H A Haywood (undated)

Acquired at the Museum of Garden
   History, London 1994

Watercolour on paper 330 x 180 mm

WILD CABBAGE

Signed H A Haywood 1994

Acquired at the Museum of Garden
   History, London 1994

Watercolour on paper 723 x 525 mm

SUE HERBERT

BORN DARWEN, ENGLAND 1954

One of the first paintings I saw at the Hunt Institute's 7th International Exhibition in 1992 was an enormous leaf that was most arresting in its stark simplicity.

I asked Sue Herbert, who lives and works in London, to show me more of her paintings and she arrived with a huge portfolio of 'king-sized' leaf portraits. The leaves had been culled from river banks and pressed. She had painted them when they were partially dried out and they looked exactly like specimens in a herbarium. It is interesting that every artist who sees my collection has always been attracted to this subject.

Sue Herbert trained at the Sunderland College of Art and graduated in 1976. She has contributed to exhibitions at the Society of Botanical Artists, the Society of Wildlife Artists and at the Chelsea Physic Garden, London.

LEAF

Signed Susan Herbert (undated)

Acquired from the artist 1992

Watercolour on paper 690 x 460 mm

JEANNE HOLGATE

BORN LONDON 1920

With a career as one of the world's leading botanical painters, spanning at least 40 years, Jeanne Holgate has divided her time between England and the United States. Indeed, when I kept hearing about her in relation to Longwood Gardens, Pennsylvania, where she taught in the 1960s, I thought she must be American.

During World War II she joined the Women's Auxiliary Air Force and attained the rank of flight officer. She taught herself flower painting and became an official artist to the RHS from 1954 to 1966. The society has over five hundred of her orchid paintings. She was awarded four gold medals and won the silver trophy for best scientific exhibition with her work on orchids at the 4th World Orchid Conference.

She moved from England in 1966 and began her connection with Longwood, one of the most important and impressive gardens in the United States which has been wonderfully supported by the Dupont family. I well remember having dinner in one of its immaculate and towering conservatories, with the formal gardens stretched around us as far as the eye could see.

She has had one-person shows at Sotheby's and the British Museum in London and all over the United States, while the Hunt Institute held a retrospective of her work in 1973.

In 1972 she was commissioned to paint 'The Flowers of America', showing each state's flower emblem. This was a mammoth task, resulting in a large (560 x 710 mm/22 x 28 inch) limited portfolio. To complete it she travelled over 45,000 kilometres (28,000 miles) from Maine to Hawaii, and from Alaska to New Mexico, taking over four years in the process. She is held in many collections including those of HM Elizabeth the Queen Mother, the Hunt Institute, the British Museum and the University of North Carolina, and is illustrated in *The art of botanical illustration* by Wilfrid Blunt and William T. Stearn (1994) with a wonderful portrait of a pale pink magnolia. She is a founder member of the Guild of Scientific Illustrators, and was elected a Fellow of the Linnean Society in 1991.

I wandered into Hal O'Nians' gallery in St James's, London, in 1991, less than a year after I had started collecting, and was immediately captivated by a lovely painting of a yellow peony. When I spoke to Jeanne Holgate about it she told me she particularly remembered painting the red veining in the stem and along the leaves, something that is distinctive to that plant and quite beautifully observed in the illustration here.

PAEONIA MLOKOSEWITSCHII

Signed Jeanne Holgate (undated)

Acquired from King Street Galleries, London 1991

Watercolour on paper 240 x 340 mm

Jeanne Holgate.

MARIKO IMAI

BORN TANAGAWA, JAPAN 1942

Mariko Imai is considered to be one of the best botanical artists in Japan and I thought it was important to visit her. She was holding a small exhibition in the hallway of an office building (exhibitions are often held in commercial premises or in department stores in Japan) in Mito, some considerable distance from Tokyo. I set off with my trusty Japanese colleague, Keiko Saino, who navigated me through two train trips and then translated for me when I finally met Imai. She was wearing practical corduroy trousers and tough boots and looked as if she was just off for a hike in the countryside.

She has had many solo and joint exhibitions, both in Japan and Canada, and illustrated a great number of books including quite a few for children. In 1992 and 1993 her paintings were used on the covers of the journal produced by the Japanese branch of the RHS. She has taught at art school, lectured at botanical gardens and, like so many other good botanical artists, has spent some time working as a textile designer.

Her favourite subjects are the orchid genera *Masdevallia* and *Dracula* and most of the paintings in her exhibition were of these plants. There were a few more stylized, less finished illustrations which she had used for covers on botanical magazines. I eventually chose *Heterotropa muramatsui* for its strong design element and intriguing mass of tangled roots.

A recent publication, *Masdevallia and Dracula,* has some superb illustrations by Imai, beautifully reproduced. Her sense of composition is unerring and her leaf texture particularly well painted.

HETEROTROPA MURAMATSUI

Signed Imai (undated)

Acquired from the artist 1994

Watercolour on paper 380 x 250 mm

PAUL JONES

BORN SYDNEY, AUSTRALIA 1921

Paul Jones is by far the best known flower painter in Australia, whose exquisitely beautiful work is celebrated in several important books and has been collected worldwide.

He trained at East Sydney Technical College and at the Julian Ashton Art School. He was first interested in camellias and produced superb plates for *The camellia* in two volumes published by the Leslie Urquhart Press, London (with a few plates by Raymond Booth). Then came the two limited edition books, *Flora superba* and *Flora magnifica*, published by the Tryon Gallery, London, where the original paintings were also exhibited to great acclaim.

He was awarded the OBE for his services to art in 1971.

He visited Japan in the mid-1970s and when he returned to Australia felt much influenced by the work he had seen there. It was then that he painted *Camellia* 'Paul Jones Supreme', the camellia named after him.

For three summers in the 1980s he visited West Green, Hampshire, England, to paint a set of 40 flower portraits from plants growing in Lord McAlpine's garden. I saw them hanging there on the occasion of Alistair's 40th birthday. Paul Jones painted *Romneya trichocalyx* from the garden in 1988 and 1989. He told me how he had been eagerly waiting for the main bud to open so that he could paint a really choice bloom; and was devastated to find the next morning that someone going round the garden on the open day had stolen it and taken several buds as well. So that is why the portrait was painted over two years.

When I started collecting botanical paintings I visited Lord McAlpine's gallery in Cork Street, London, and fought my way through his extraordinarily eclectic mixture of artefacts (he collects Roman and Celtic objects, Australian aboriginal bark paintings, coins, dinosaur eggs and much else besides). There I found a number of Paul Jones' paintings nestling alongside Sidney Nolan's massive canvases and chose the two shown here.

I arranged to meet him recently in Sydney, where he lives in a delightful studio house with a small garden in the rear. Now in his seventies, he seems to be doing very little flower painting, but is concentrating on black-and-white photography. He does every stage of the photographic development himself so that he can get exactly the result he wants.

These pictures are amongst the most remarkable flower

CAMELLIA 'PAUL JONES SUPREME'

Signed Paul Jones '77

Acquired from Erasmus Gallery, London 1991

Acrylic on paper 512 x 330 mm

CALIFORNIAN
TREE POPPY:
*ROMNEYA
TRICHOCALYX*

Signed Paul Jones
(painted 1988–89)

Acquired from Erasmus
Gallery, London 1991

Acrylic on paper
710 x 520 mm

*CAMELLIA
JAPONICA*
'USU-OTOME'

Signed Paul Jones (undated)

Gift from the artist 1995

Watercolour on paper
190 x 180 mm

photographs I have ever seen, created by a man who truly appreciates the subtlety and beauty of flowers.

He describes himself as a flower painter, not a botanical illustrator, and is quite right to do so. His work has a romantic and dramatic appeal which is often not found in scientific illustration; yet he does not sacrifice accuracy in his work: he always gets a great 'feel' for each subject.

When I was visiting him he showed me his remark-able shell collection, a passion he has indulged for much of his life. The shells are all labelled and exquisitely arranged in subtle patterns in drawer after drawer. I was overwhelmed by his treasures and I suppose rather surprised, in retrospect, that he had not portrayed more shells in his work. He did, however, use them in the design of a beautiful set of postage stamps for Papua New Guinea in the 1980s.

ANNETTE DE JONQUIERES

BORN COPENHAGEN, DENMARK 1942

Although she is now living in Denmark again, Annette de Jonquières was first inspired by the work of Margaret Mee in Brazil. At the time she was living in São Paulo and saw Mee's paintings in a friend's collection. She saw bromeliads and orchids similar to those that Margaret Mee had painted growing around her and started drawing herself. She had no formal training except for two weeks of classes at Kew.

I met Annette in Bangkok, before I had really started collecting seriously. She was a wonderful companion, exploring the klongs, foraging in antique shops, trying unusual food; in fact she was fascinated by everything in that throbbing, exciting and exhausting city.

I asked her to paint me some of the local water plants for use as illustrations in my new magazine based on South-east Asia. She foraged through the klongs, picking lotus, water lilies and the last of that season's water-hyacinth blooms.

She had one-person shows in São Paulo and at the Oriental Hotel in Bangkok. She was represented in the Hunt Institute's 8th International Exhibition in 1995, where she showed an excellent *Amaryllis* which is now part of the Hunt's collection. She is doing illustrations for *The Danish encyclopedia* and produces a range of charming postcards.

I have a dramatic painting of a bromeliad executed while she was in Bangkok and a more recent study of a wild strawberry which she has used for a postcard illustration.

WILD STRAWBERRY

Signed Annette de Jonquières, *Fragaria vesca*, juli 1995

Acquired from the artist 1995

Watercolour on paper 480 x 360 mm

Fragaria vesca
Kbh., juli 1995 Annettede Jonguières©

SALLY KEIR

As with so many women painters, Sally Keir did not start her artistic career until she was in her mid-forties because of family commitments. She took a degree in design, specializing in jewellery and silversmithing, at Duncan of Jordanstone College, Dundee. At the same time she started painting, initially in watercolour but graduating to gouache to give the more intense and dramatic jewel-tones that make her flowers glow from a dark background. Since 1985 she has also worked as a lecturer in metalwork.

She was awarded a number of medals by the RHS in the early 1990s and has shown widely in Britain and abroad. I saw her work at the Hunt Institute and was interested in its intensity and the way she had achieved depth and fleshy texture through shadows. It is quite different from anything else in my collection.

PINK RHODODENDRON

Signed SAK (undated) Pink Rhododendron

Acquired from the artist 1994

Gouache on board 330 x 380 mm

SAK

Pink Rhodode

CHRISTABEL KING

BORN LONDON 1950

Christabel King is a quiet, meticulous painter who draws the best cactus portraits in the world. She paints other plants beautifully too, but I feel she particularly excells at cacti, perfectly capturing the weird contrast of their delicate flowers and fat succulent stems bedecked with wicked spines. She inherited her father's collection of cacti plants and now grows her own, painting the flowers at their brief moment of perfection.

She is a freelance botanical artist who has been closely associated with Kew since 1975, producing a series of superb paintings published in *Curtis's Botanical Magazine* and she received the Jill Smythies Award for Botanical Illustration from the Linnean Society in 1989. She teaches part-time at Capel Manor Horticultural and Environmental Centre at Enfield.

She has also had great influence tutoring student artists sent to Kew with help from the Margaret Mee Amazon Trust scholarship scheme whom she started teaching in 1990. I was amazed to see the improvement in botanical painting in Brazil over the last few years and feel that much is due to her patient dedication. She recently visited Brazil to be fêted by her students, and had the most stimulating and exciting time in the Amazon, holding seminars in the jungle.

She has been involved with other overseas exploration. In 1987 she was part of an expedition to Uganda to paint the unique and extraordinary flora of the Ruwenzori Mountains, to illustrate Guy Yeoman's book *Africa's mountains of the moon,* where she also sketched landscapes. Closer to home, she has illustrated three Kew Magazine monographs on *Pleione, Echinocereus* and *Lewisia*: a fourth monograph on *Cleistocactus* is in progress.

I was most impressed with her painting of the showy tree *Spathodea*, which was one of the highlights of her exhibition at Kew Gardens Gallery. I bought it and commissioned her to do any cactus of her choice. When she showed me the small, delicate, shell-pink flower of *Gymnocalycium* cf. *fleischerianum* I immediately realized that it would become one of the gems of my collection. The cushiony, fat stem was in perfect contrast to the fragile, transient bloom.

She has produced a great body of superb work in the last few years and must be considered one of today's best botanical illustrators.

GYMNOCALYCIUM cf. FLEISCHERIANUM

Signed C F King

Labelled: *Gymnocalycium* cf. *fleischerianum*

Cult C F King 6/8/92

Commissioned 1993

Watercolour on paper 210 x 170 mm

AFRICAN TULIP TREE: *SPATHODEA COMPANULATA* VAR. *NILOTICA*

Signed C F King, Jan. 1993

Labelled: Uganda: Ruwenzori Mts., Nyakalingeju, 1600 m, CFK 324, tree in riverside forest. 16/8/87; fruit drawn from J. Lebrun 9383, Ruindi, Zaire

Acquired from Kew Gardens Gallery 1993

Watercolour on paper 265 x 365 mm

CHARLOTTE KNOX

BORN LONDON 1951

Despite the fact that she lives and works in London I first saw Charlotte Knox's decorative work at Ursus Prints, New York, in 1992. The gallery was showing a set of paintings she had done to illustrate *Fruit* and *Seafood* by Alan Davidson.

She trained at the Ruskin School of Fine Art, Oxford, and then did a postgraduate course in illustration at St Martin's College of Art and Design in London. She was a worthy winner of the W.H. Smith award for illustration held at the Victoria & Albert Museum in 1992 and a set of autumn postage stamps she was commissioned to do for the Royal Mail was voted the most popular set for 1993. She was working on these when I visited her studio and I admired her strong sense of design and clarity of execution.

Charlotte Knox's illustrations are so appealing that it is easy to understand why she is getting so many commissions for stamps and books.

OTAHEITE GOOSEBERRY, EMBLIC, BIGNAY AND RAMBAI

Signed Charlotte Knox 1991

Acquired from Ursus Prints, Madison Avenue, New York, 1992

Watercolour on paper 305 x 240 mm

Reproduced in *Fruit* by Alan Davidson
and Charlotte Knox p. 127

Left to right: Otaheite gooseberries with yellow fruit,
bignays with red, yellow and purple fruit, emblics with green fruit, rambais
with yellow-brown fruit.

MARIKO KOJIMA

BORN HOTEN, CHINA 1937

Mariko Kojima is one of Japan's most established and well-known botanical artists, who now lives in Kanagawa. She trained with Yowai Ota and Yoshio Futakuchi (a most respected teacher, now in his nineties, who has recently produced a book of gentle camellia paintings). She has been an active member of the Japan Botanical Art Association, helping to organize the last eight of their annual exhibitions. In addition she teaches at the Sankei Academy, Tokyo, and at several other cultural centres. She has been commissioned to execute several sets of stamps including a 'Cherry Blossom' series in 1990.

I first saw her work at the Hunt Institute's 7th International Exhibition where she was showing a most beautiful orchid. I wrote to her in English, only realizing later how difficult it would be to communicate with artists in Japan. Eventually I was able to get my letter translated into Japanese characters and, in turn, have her reply interpreted for me. She sent me some of her postcards and a newspaper cutting which showed her painting a strawberry plant which I thought looked interesting. It took me several months to establish satisfactory contact and for the arrival of the strawberry plant painting, but I have enjoyed it ever since.

Her ripe strawberries are plump and inviting and the green developing fruits are beautifully painted.

I met her when I visited Tokyo in the spring of 1994. Having seen more of her work I commissioned her to paint one of the roses she was cultivating in her garden and it duly arrived after the flowering season.

STRAWBERRIES

Signed Mari (undated)

Acquired from the artist 1992

Watercolour on paper 380 x 250 mm

VIET MARTIN KUNZ

BORN STUTTGART, GERMANY 1941

Kunz started his career as an art teacher after graduating from Stuttgart. He has concentrated on botanical illustrations in watercolour from 1972, showing solo in Filderstadt Municipal Gallery, in Bad Wörishofen and Wilhelma Zoological and Botanical Garden in Stuttgart in 1990.

He showed at the 7th International Exhibition at the Hunt Institute in 1992 and it was there that I first saw his work. I liked and purchased his 'Brussels Sprouts' and later bought an illustration of an *Eryngium* thistle that he had painted on the Atlantic shore when he was on holiday, which he called 'Sand Thistle'.

SAND THISTLE: *ERYNGIUM MARITIMUM*

Signed V.M. Kunz (undated)

Acquired from the artist 1992

Watercolour on paper 390 x 340 mm

VM Kunz

JOANNA ASQUITH LANGHORNE

BORN FULMER CHASE, ENGLAND 1945

Encouraged by her father, himself an artist, Joanna Langhorne attended several field study courses at Flatford Mill, Essex, where she was tutored by John Nash and, later, Mary Grierson.

This triggered a long and fruitful career in botanical painting. She studied graphic design for a BA degree and then worked at the Freshwater Biological Association as a zoological illustrator. In 1973 she was appointed to a full-time post as official artist in residence at Kew and stayed there until 1980.

She has a illustrated a number of monographs, executing over 80 plates for *Curtis's Botanical Magazine*, and with work in many other publications. She has had half a dozen solo exhibitions including shows at the RHS, the Chelsea Physic Garden and the British Museum, and over 30 where she has exhibited with other artists.

I liked her work when I saw it in 'Three Continents', an exhibition at Kew Gardens Gallery in 1993. She showed a delightful painting of slipper orchids which had been used as a frontispiece for an issue of *The Plantsman* and a beautifully painted mountain ash, with the berries and leaves glowing with autumn light.

MOUNTAIN ASH: *SORBUS AUCUPARIA*

Signed Joanna A. Langhorne (undated)

Acquired from Kew Gardens Gallery 1993

Watercolour on paper 285 x 305 mm

Joanna A. Langhorne

KATIE LEE

BORN ELDORET, KENYA 1942

Born in Kenya, Africa, Katie Lee is the daughter of a British colonial policeman. She is now an American citizen although some of her family still live in England and she spent most of her childhood there. She trained at the New York Botanical Garden Botanical Illustration Programme from 1989 to 1991 and developed a realistic and well-designed style of considerable appeal.

Since then she has been teaching at the New York Botanical Garden and has illustrated a number of books. She shows her work at Ursus Prints, Madison Avenue, New York, at the Silo Gallery, New Milford, Connecticut, and at Wave Hill, New York. She is represented at the Hunt Institute, has been in group shows with the Guild of Natural Science Illustrators and received a merit award at the Don Harrington Discovery Centre in 1993.

Her book illustrations are very appealing and she has recently published a particularly charming book, *A visit to Galápagos*. She feels very strongly about preserving the integrity of the ecosystem, something that was reinforced by her first visit there when she sat, surrounded by sea lions, with Sally Lightfoot crabs scrambling over the sand.

I first met her when she was dismantling a small show at the New York Botanical Garden and I bought a charming painting of a *Streptocarpus*. On a later occasion I drove out to her home in South Salem to see her working space and meet her properly.

Hanging in her living room was a yellow orchid which she had painted on a trip to the Rio Negro in Brazil. Its long, trailing, almost root-like leaves were very familiar and I eventually realized that I had seen the same subject painted by Margaret Mee. In Mee's book *In search of flowers of the Amazon forests* (1988) she tells how she found *Scuticaria steelii* bordering a creek on the River Daraá, Rio Negro. Katie's specimen certainly looks identical to Margaret Mee's.

Katie described how she collected and painted it:

'We were on the Rio Negro – best actual location we all can come up with is two hours out of Manaus. Our guide Mo would just go-go, and no matter how we tried to follow our daily locations on a map it proved impossible. The evening was crystal clear, we had just returned from a two-day hike and sleeping out in the jungle, and a few of us went out in one of the small boats. I had decided to leave my camera behind in order to just do visual inputting. The area was still, black water with dead tree trunks emerging. As the sun began to set, the moon rose in competition on the other horizon, the reflections of the tree trunks were straight up and down – giving the impression of very tall trees, the junction of water to tree completely lost. Almost all of the trees were draped with orchids and bromeliads of all kinds. So pure black was the water, and perfect the reflection it was hard not to be tempted to reach into the water to touch the blossoms. One of our party, Scott Mori, had a collecting licence, so Mo climbed a trunk and got the orchid – rotten branch and all. Heaven, pure heaven. This is when I really envied Margaret Mee, and made a promise to myself that as soon as possible I would spend more and more time in these places, drawing. The light was gone by the time we returned to the boat, so the next day I sketched and photographed – it was the first painting I did when I got home. The first study painted on returning from a trip is always the best – most energetic and most truthful.'

As a commission she painted me the dogwood *Cornus florida* early one year. I have always found it the most striking and beautiful tree in the American woods, heralding the spring. Another lovely study is one of Iceland poppies whose soft colours she has captured to perfection.

SCUTICARIA STEELII

Signed KT 1991 collected Rio Negro, Amazonas

Acquired from the artist 1992

Gouache on Stonehenge Print 140 lb HP 740 x 350 mm

DOGWOOD: *CORNUS FLORIDA*

Signed KT 1993

Acquired from the artist 1993

Gouache on Stonehenge Print 560 x 380 mm

ICELAND POPPIES: *PAPAVER NUDICAULE*

Signed KT 1992

Acquired from the artist 1993

Gouache on Whatman 140 lb HP 325 x 340 mm

THALIA LINCOLN

BORN CAPE TOWN, SOUTH AFRICA 1924

Thalia Lincoln trained at the Michaelis School of Fine Art in Cape Town and then worked for a time in advertising and at the Olifantsfontein Pottery Studio, applying designs on to pottery.

It was in 1964, when she was in her forties, that she started drawing flowers. When I first saw some of her excellent colour prints of native South African plants I assumed that she used watercolour but closer examination, and a visit to her home, made me realize that she achieved her results by using layer upon layer of dry coloured pencil, to build up an intense colour base with fine detail and shadow being put in with graphite pencil. This painstaking and very lengthy process eventually produced some of the most magnificent portraits of the native proteas.

In 1975 she started a major project with Dr John Rourke, Curator of the Compton Herbarium, National Botanic Gardens, Kirstenbosch. They collaborated on a definitive study of the genera *Mimetes* and *Orothamnus*, with Thalia illustrating the flowers set against each plant's authentic habitat. These rare plants, which belong to the protea family, only grow in the Cape, often in very restricted and inaccessible places, and many are immensely difficult to propagate. Each one had to be tracked down and sketched in the wild at its moment of flowering. It took years of fieldwork, expeditions to remote places and then concentrated work in her studio before Thalia finally finished the project. The result was a fine monograph, illustrated with beautifully reproduced plates of mimetes flowering on the hillsides, often towering above the other native plants. The book *Mimetes* was a limited edition but can be found in some botanic libraries, including Kew.

In 1989 she was commissioned by Sappi (South African Pulp and Paper Industries) to draw indigenous South African flowers for a Sappi portfolio. A limited number of signed prints are produced by a particular artist each year and the proceeds go towards the World Wildlife Fund.

Many other artists like Raymond Ching and David Shepherd have been asked to do comparable series of about a dozen plates in total, always on African subjects.

When I met Thalia in 1990 she was already preoccupied with the Sappi project and reluctant to do anything else; although she did show me some curious, abstract drawings of concentric rings which I never completely understood, but which apparently had some occult significance. Over the last few years she has seemed a rather small figure, frail and unwell and having trouble with her drawing wrist.

In the end I despaired of getting a protea drawing from her and opted to buy one from the Sappi portfolio when it was at last completed in 1995. Only a few of her 12 drawings were available and I chose *Zantedeschia pentlandii*, a spectacular arum lily with a chrome-yellow spathe marked with a dramatic dark purple blotch in its centre. It has a restricted natural distribution in the Eastern Transvaal where it is found on rocky ground near streams on the grassy mountainside in the Belfast and Lydenburg districts. It flowers during the South African summer, in November and December, and dies down completely in the cold months. It makes a spectacular pot plant and I have every intention of trying to grow it soon. My drawing was on display with the rest of the Sappi portfolio in South Africa and London during the last part of 1995.

There is no doubt that Thalia Lincoln is among the very best of South African flower artists and some of her portraits of proteas, agapanthus and lilies in particular are breathtaking in their beauty. Signed prints can be bought at Kirstenbosch botanical gardens, Cape Town. Thalia has supervised the reproduction and it is very good.

CALLA LILY: *ZANTEDESCHIA PENTLANDII*

Signed Thalia Lincoln (undated)

Acquired from Everard Read Gallery, Johannesburg 1995

Coloured pencil on paper 590 x 470 mm

Zantedeschia penttandii

PETR LISKA

BORN PRAGUE, CZECH REPUBLIC 1953

Petr Liška trained between 1968 and 1972 at the High School of Graphic Arts in Prague. In 1980 he became head of the publicity department at the Medical Plants Company in the same city and created designs and illustrations for a variety of printed material. Since 1991 he has worked as a freelance artist. He works in tempera and his paintings have been reproduced in a number of Czech magazines. His work was exhibited in the 6th International Exhibition at the Hunt Institute in 1988, and at the Everard Read Gallery in Johannesburg. His illustrations have appeared in several books including *The illustrated guide to cacti* by Rudolf Slaba (1992), *Les fruits* by Dlouhá, Richter & Valícek (1995) and *Le Jardin de rocaille* by V. Vodicková (1995).

I visited his apartment on the outskirts of Prague. He showed me some small paintings in acrylic on paper, sitting in his tidy, well-organized studio-room lined with the books he has illustrated.

The painting of *Aporocactus flagelliformis*, the rat's-tail cactus from Mexico, shown here with its trailing stems and upright flowers is painted from the same plant that appeared in *The illustrated guide to cacti*. Another, the tiny, white *Rebutia narvaezensis*, is the actual painting for the book. I could not resist the plums with their beautifully painted bloom, nor the small *Carlina acaulis*.

APOROCACTUS FLAGELLIFORMIS

Signed Liška '95

Acquired from the artist 1995

Acrylic on paper 250 x 175 mm

STEMLESS THISTLE: *CARLINA ACAULIS*

Signed Liška '93

Acquired from the artist 1994

Acrylic on paper 210 x 150 mm

REBUTIA NARVAEZENSIS

Signed Liška '88, reproduced on page 198 of *The illustrated guide to cacti* by R. Slaba

Gift from the artist 1995

Acrylic on paper 250 x 175 mm

RORY McEWEN

I believe that Rory McEwen's work influenced the development of a number of artists in my collection; Brigid Edwards, Jenny Brasier, Susannah Blaxhill and Lindsay Megarrity are examples. I had seen some of his paintings in reproduction, but it was only recently, when I saw the true scale of them, that I realized the profound impact of his unique vision.

I regret that I never met him, nor did I go to the memorial exhibition of his work in Scotland and at the Serpentine Gallery, London, in 1988. But I do know some of his family and have recently met his widow, Romana McEwen. She allowed me to look through his paintings and at last get a feeling for the originals.

It is particularly important to see McEwen's original work, for although he painted many flowers such as his carnation and auricula series to scale, and with the intense observation and detail needed for botanical identification, he also painted other plant subjects quite differently. The crown imperial shown here is about one and a quarter times larger than the natural plant, giving great drama to the painting. He floated leaves and flowers ethereally in space, sometimes enlarging them tenfold to fill his frame, sometimes arranging them in horizontal order isolated on a huge piece of vellum. These paintings are as signficant for their space as for their subjects.

His friends have all told me that he was a man of great gifts, a jazz player, a poet, immensely charming. He travelled widely, especially in the Far East, and showed his work in Japan and also in a number of modern art galleries. He painted flowers from the age of eight and was encouraged by Wilfrid Blunt, his art teacher at Eton, to look at the works of Redouté and Ehret. Blunt described him as, 'perhaps the most gifted artist to pass through my hands'. It was particularly disappointing to find that McEwen, who had featured prominently in Blunt's first edition of *The art of botanical illustration,* should not even rate a mention in the second edition.

He had no formal training at an art school, but by the time he finished at Cambridge University his illustrations had been published in *Old carnations and pinks* by Charles Oscar Moreton (1955). He illustrated *The auricula* in 1964, and painted many of the plates for Wilfrid Blunt's *Tulips and tulipomania* (1977).

John McEwen, Rory's youngest brother, writes:

'The greatest change in Rory's work in the 1960s was to discard paper for vellum. The best quality vellum, made from the hides of unborn kids, was still procurable. Vellum was the product of an art in itself and Rory responded to its challenge. No paper can match the smoothness of its surface or lend such translucency and richness to watercolour. Rory painted on it with the concentration of a watchmaker, using a sheaf of the tiniest sable brushes, a sheet of cartridge paper as a colour tester and a delicate pen-knife to scrape away any errors. He painted from cut specimens, sometimes lying them alongside the board on which he stretched the skin as tight as a drum. His long experiment with the relation of subject and space now began. In 1963 he introduced two or more subjects in a single image.

'Rory's role as a folk-singer, television producer and concert promoter interrupted his painting until 1964, when he stopped playing the guitar professionally. But it did not prevent his evolution from a documentary to an imaginative painter, the key difference between the botanical illustrator and the floral artist. With the botanical masters – for Rory the likes of Robert, Redouté, Ehret and Aubriet – description and imagination co-exist. Rory's work in the 1950s always displayed a poetic refinement,

CROWN IMPERIAL:
FRITILLARIA IMPERIALIS

Signed Rory McEwen 1965

Acquired from private collection 1995

Watercolour on vellum 780 x 565 mm

Rory McEwen
1965

even if it purposely inclined to traditional illustration, but he aspired to be a modern artist.

'During the early 1970s he embarked on a series entitled 'True Facts from Nature'. Plants were often mixed with vegetables and placed sequentially with the accent on spatial tension. Desiccated plants and dead leaves are depicted for the first time. Sentiment was implicit in the choice of subject. Many are reminders of his childhood – catching falling leaves for luck was an autumn ritual – or have other emotional significances. Desiccation itself, the fading of glory, seems to reflect the onset of his own middle age.

'In the final months Rory experimented even more daringly by painting similarly detailed watercolours on vellum of the magnified heads of some his favourite flowers – the fritillary (also a favourite butterfly of his) and the gentian.

Douglas Hall, founder and first keeper of the Scottish Gallery of Modern Art, has written: "His position is assured as a highly aware modern artist in an ancient tradition." Rory's mission was accomplished.'

Having longed to add one of his later paintings to my collection I was delighted when I at last obtained this beautiful work 'Summer 1974. Old Fashioned Rose, Beech Mast and Clover', derived from his series 'True Facts from Nature'. The old-fashioned rose shows his mastery of watercolour on vellum, while the composition itself seems as much about the surrounding space as the three objects suspended there.

SUMMER 1974. OLD FASHIONED ROSE, BEECH MAST AND CLOVER

Signed Rory McEwen, painted 1974

Acquired from the McEwen Estate 1995

Watercolour on vellum 545 x 695 mm

KATHERINE MANISCO

BORN UNITED KINGDOM 1935

Although she now lives in New York, Katherine Manisco is still a British citizen. She trained at the Slade School of Fine Art, London, and later at the Accademia di Firenze in Italy and was art director for Wells, Rich & Greene for ten years from 1977.

She exhibited at the Hunt Institute's 7th International Exhibition in 1992 and has had several shows in New York. I saw her work at the Horticultural Society of New York in 1992 and bought a watercolour and pencil drawing of a sunflower. Later she showed at the RHS and still more recently I saw a portfolio of new work which she had brought over to London. One of these new paintings has been included in the permanent collection of the Victoria & Albert Museum, London.

I was interested to see a substantial change in her style and bought a lovely study of the tulip tree. She has observed most subtle changes in the leaf colour and the whole painting is beautifully placed upon the page. She collected this specimen in Old Westbury Gardens, Long Island, New York. She saw a superb tulip tree and took some branches back to her studio in Milbrook, Pine Plains, New York, to work on the painting while they were still fresh. I am particularly attracted to the tulip tree with its subtle yellow, green and orange bell-shaped flowers which I first saw in profusion covering the paths in Pam Dupont Copeland's famous garden 'Cuba' in Delaware in the United States one spring. The carpet of flowers had fallen from the tree canopy far above. Inspired, I planted some trees in my country garden, but they have a long way to grow to rival the American specimens.

TULIP TREE: *LIRIODENDRON TULIPIFERA*

Signed Katherine Manisco 1995

Acquired from the artist 1995

Watercolour on paper 475 x 390 mm

KATHERINE MANISCO
PO BOX 560 PINE PLAINS NEW YORK 12567

TEL 914 868 7290   FAX 914 868 7473

KATHERINE MANISCO IS A GRADUATE OF THE SLADE SCHOOL OF ART, LONDON UNIVERSITY.   SHE ALSO STUDIED PAINTING AT THE ACCADEMIA IN FLORENCE AND IS A MEMBER OF THE AMERICAN SOCIETY OF BOTANICAL PAINTERS.

HER WORK IS INCLUDED IN THE PERMANENT COLLECTIONS OF THE VICTORIA & ALBERT MUSEUM, THE FITZWILLIAM MUSEUM AND THE HUNT INSTITUTE FOR BOTANICAL DOCUMENTATION, CARNEGIE MELLON UNIVERSITY.   SHE IS LISTED IN THE HUNT INSTITUTE'S SEVENTH INTERNATIONAL CATALOGUE OF BOTANICAL ART AND ILLUSTRATION.

HER WATERCOLORS WERE SHOWN AT A ONE WOMAN EXHIBITION IN THE FALL OF 1992 AT THE HORTICULTURAL SOCIETY OF NEW YORK, AND AT THE ROYAL HORTICULTURAL SOCIETY IN LONDON IN FEBRUARY, 1993, WHEN SHE WAS AWARDED THE GRENFELL MEDAL FOR BOTANICAL ILLUSTRATION.

A COLLECTION OF HER WATERCOLORS WAS EXHIBITED IN NOVEMBER, 1993, AT THE STUBBS GALLERY IN NEW YORK CITY.   HER WORK HAS ALSO BEEN FEATURED IN ELLE DECOR AND NEW YORK MAGAZINE.

HER BOTANICAL PAINTINGS ARE IN A NUMBER OF PRIVATE COLLECTIONS IN EUROPE AND THE UNITED STATES.

JOHN MORGAN MATYAS

BORN OHIO, USA 1955

Here is an artist whose passion for tropical rain-forests has led to an extensive commitment to conservation. He has been preparing an impor-tant and enormous portfolio of endangered plants and animals of Costa Rica's rainforest, *In the realm of Eden: an artist in the rain forest*. This will be exhibited in many venues starting in Washington DC in 1996.

Matyas lectures about the environment to encourage conservation through education. He has been commis-sioned by several organizations which support rainforest studies. Since 1980 he has had many solo exhibitions.

His huge painting of the ostrich fern dominated the 7th International Exhibition at the Hunt Institute in 1992. I found his work strong and well designed and eventually bought a painting of a bromeliad with its flower just about to be pollinated by a humming-bird which is searching for nectar. He wrote to me about this painting which he titled 'Sizing Up':

'It depicts one of the most beautiful bromeliads of South America, *Vriesea mariae*. Its brilliant red and char-treuse inflorescence (which can last for several months) is easily targeted in this world of green by the humming-birds that frequent the humid lower canopy layers between 30–60 metres high.

A colleague in Ecuador sent a specimen of *Topaza pella*, the crimson topaz humming-bird, to my studio for use in this painting so that I could show the actual size compar-ison between flower and bird. In the rain forest, *Topaza pella* not only feasts on nectar and small insects located in the inflorescence but also assists in pollinating the small flowers found within the vibrant bracts. By utilizing a combination of transparent and opaque watercolours I am able to bring out the subtle graying effect on the leaves of the bromeliad due to the growth of fungus on them and still display the exciting colours of the inflorescence and humming-bird.'

'SIZING UP': *VRIESEA MARIAE*
WITH *TOPAZA PELLA*

Signed J.M. Matyas 1990

Labelled: 'Sizing Up'

Acquired from the artist 1994

Watercolour and gouache on paper 860 x 740 mm

MARGARET MEE

BORN CHESHAM, ENGLAND; 1909–1988

Margaret Mee trained as an artist in London at St Martin's School of Art, Central Art School and Camberwell School of Art. In the early 1950s she moved to Brazil with her husband: here she taught art but by 1958 she had begun to paint the native flowers for which she became renowned.

One of my greatest regrets while making this collection was that I never met Margaret Mee. It is true that I did not start collecting seriously until 1990 and by that time she had already died, not in one of her daring and lonely trips to the Amazon, but tragically in a car accident near Leicester, in England, only a few weeks after her triumphant exhibition at Kew had opened. But our paths had nearly crossed several times earlier in Rio de Janeiro, where we had mutual friends in Mario and Julia Gibson-Barbosa. Mario now heads up the Fundação Margaret Mee in Brazil and I am involved with the sister foundation in the United Kingdom which raises money to fund the exchange of scholars between Kew and Brazil.

I bought my first three paintings in Rio from a number shown to me by Sylvia de Brautigam, owned by Margaret Mee's husband, Greville. They were early works; indeed one is almost certainly the first plant she painted in the Amazon in 1956. She describes in her autobiography how she visited the Botanical Garden Museu Goeldi in Belém and asked someone to cut down a flowering branch of the cannonball tree and the date fits exactly. There is a vigour and immediacy in her early work which I find most attractive, although she probably painted leaves with more subtlety later on. I bought three more paintings on later visits to Rio and two from the Tryon Gallery which had shown her work in London in the 1970s and 1980s. One painting from the Tryon Gallery was a philodendron set against a backdrop of rainforest trees. She painted only about a dozen scenes with backgrounds from the Amazon, each with a full-scale rainforest flower in the front. Greville Mee told me that she really did not care for these paintings as much as for her more classic studies. But it is these paintings with their jungly settings that have caught the public imagination and are reproduced far more than her other work.

She was a remarkable woman, apparently frail and delicate with a mass of wavy gold hair who survived 15 arduous trips to the Amazon, usually with only local Indian guides. Hers was one of the first warning voices decrying the destruction of the rainforest. Some of the flowers she painted have not been seen again and their habitat has been destroyed by the relentless advance of slash-and-burn farming, logging and gold mining. She discovered a number of previously unknown species, of which four are named after her, and she brought back hundreds of valuable plants which were then cultivated in the Rio Botanical Gardens or by the landscape architect, Roberto Burle Marx.

I was invited to have lunch with Roberto Burle Marx in his remarkable house some 20 kilometres (12 miles) outside Rio. He had 18 paintings by Margaret Mee that I particularly wanted to see. Some were of plants she had brought back and had been named after him. Here he kept his amazing nursery of plants, some of which he had

CANNONBALL TREE:
COUROUPITA GUIANENSIS

Signed Margaret Mee (undated)

Couroupita guianensis (J.B.) Museu Goeldi, Belém, Pará December 1956

Acquired from Greville Mee, Brazil 1990

Watercolour on paper 640 x 460 mm

Margaret Mee

Couroupita guianensis
(♀ ♂)

Museu Goeldi, Belém, Pará
December 1956

Margaret Mee

Nymphaea ampla
(Salisb.) D.C. var. pulchella Casp.

Represa de Santo Amaro
flowered July, 1957

NYMPHAEA AMPLA

Signed Margaret Mee
(undated)

Nymphaea ampla (Salisb.)
D.C. var *pulchella* Casp.
Represa de Santo Amaro,
flowered July 1957

Acquired from Greville Mee,
Brazil 1990

Watercolour on paper
630 x 460 mm

BROMELIAD NEOREGELIA SP.

Signed Margaret Mee
(undated)

Neoregelia sp. Espirito Santo

Acquired from Greville
Mee, Brazil 1992

Watercolour on paper
640 x 465 mm

introduced into cultivation while he was revolutionizing the landscaping of tropical gardens in Brazil and elsewhere around the world. I will never forget that lunch, sitting at a table spread with a cloth he had designed, beautiful tropical fish flirting in a tank nearby, the most exquisite vase of delicate jungle leaves and 80-year-old Roberto in full voice, serenading us in his splendid baritone.

Sadly he too died recently, but he left his important nursery full of rare and exotic plants to the nation.

Between them Margaret Mee and Burle Marx aroused the conscience of Brazil and the world to the depletion of the rainforest, and the Fundação Botanica Margaret Mee is still working to that end with carefully assessed grants and studentships for training today's young scientists and painters. Many have come to Kew and honed their skills with botanical artists like Christabel King and Ann Farrer.

The Fundação Botanica Margaret Mee has also started an annual competition which is exhibited in the National

PHILODENDRON

Signed Margaret Mee
(undated)

Philodendron Rio Negro
Amazonas

Acquired from Tryon
Gallery, London 1992

Watercolour on paper 640 x
470 mm

PINHEROS

Unsigned, undated and
unfinished

Acquired from and
authenticated by
Greville Mee, Brazil
1994

Watercolour on paper 620
x 450 mm

Gallery in Rio. The work of the winner is retained by the Fundação Botanica and shown in several other venues in Brazil. This year I was most impressed to see the rise in standards of the 20 competitors and the enthusiasm that has been generated. It was fascinating and heart-warming to see the dozens of small children racing around this year's Margaret Mee competition anxious to register their vote for their favourite painting – and, remarkably, their vote and that of the judges coincided for first place.

Margaret Mee produced plates for two important limited edition books, the first of which was produced in association with the Tryon Gallery. All the 58 paintings for the second one were bought recently by Kew and will be shown in a travelling exhibition in the United States over the next few years, organized by Kew and the Margaret Mee Foundation in London.

LINDSAY MEGARRITY

BORN SYDNEY, AUSTRALIA 1953

Lindsay Megarrity is one of the very few botanical artists working in Italy. He and a fellow Australian have made a wonderful nursery in the vicinity of Volterra, re-creating a garden full of herbs and roses around the old monastery of Venzano. They concentrate particularly on those that can survive the extremes of the Tuscan climate. They specialize in grey, silver and purple plants, often aromatic, that blend into the region's rolling landscape of vineyards and ancient towns.

I visited them in the autumn of 1995, driving along the winding route from Florence through the spectacular Tuscan countryside. It was glorious weather but the last few kilometres were across dirt-track roads of such complexity that navigation would have been impossible without a local guide. When we arrived for the most fleeting of visits I felt very regretful that we did not have time to explore the monastery and nursery garden properly, but I was able to commission Lindsay to paint me this autumn crocus which was just beginning to flower.

Lindsay told me that after a short and not very glorious career in the theatre he had devoted himself to botanical painting and still-life studies. He has been awarded two gold medals by the RHS, which is where I first saw his work earlier in 1995.

He was showing a series of fritillaries from Martyn Rix's collection which he has been preparing for François Coffinet Ltd, USA. He is also working on a series of antique camellia varieties for Torsanlorenzo, Rome, who also published *Fiori*, illustrated by him in 1991. Like many flower painters he works painstakingly slowly and can sell everything before it is completed, so he had little to show me in his spartan studio on the ground floor of the monastery. He has completed a number of paintings of flowers gathered in antique vases, in the style of the Dutch old masters, as well as simple flower studies. He told me that he was yet another of the painters in this collection who was inspired by Rory McEwen when he saw his memorial exhibition in 1988 at the Serpentine Gallery in London. I think this shows particularly in his studies of individual specimens.

SAFFRON: *CROCUS SATIVUS*

Signed Lindsay Megarrity 1995

Commissioned 1995

Watercolour on paper 343 x 235 mm

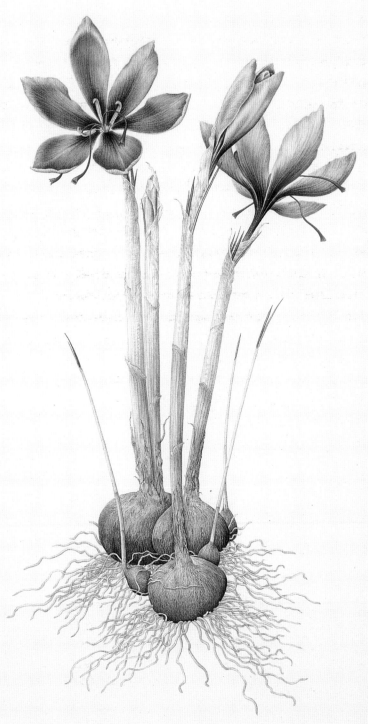

Lindsay Megarrity 1995

MITSUHARU MISHIMA

BORN TOKYO, JAPAN 1932

I met Mitsuharu Mishima in Tokyo in the spring of 1994. I had asked him to a meeting of artists at the suggestion of Mr K. Kurokawa of the Japan Botanical Art Association. It is one of two principal societies for botanical artists in Japan, the other one being called the 'Fairy Ring'.

Mishima was educated at the horticultural department of Chiba University and then at Kuwazawa Design School. From 1960 to 1962 he was a freelance graphic designer, then he became a botanical artist and was appointed botanical art tutor at Chunichi Cultural Centre. He has exhibited widely in Japan, often with the Fairy Ring, in Yokohama and Toyoma Botanical Garden. His paintings have been used as illustrations in many encyclopedias.

He is a tiny man and seemed only just larger than his paintings. He was delightfully good-humoured and insisted on both of us being photographed holding his artwork. He explained to me that he had been criticized by members of the Fairy Ring because he had not shown the tillandsia in bloom. Apparently this specimen had never come into flower properly, but he painted it and I bought it for the wonderful coils of strappy leaves entwined at its base which he has drawn to perfection.

TILLANDSIA XEROGRAPHICA

Signed M. Mishima '89 *Tillandsia xerographica*

Acquired from the artist 1994

Watercolour and pencil on paper 610 x 400 mm

M. Mishima '89

Tillandsia xerographica

KATE NESSLER

BORN ST LOUIS, MISSOURI, USA 1950

I first met Kate Nessler at one of the RHS Westminster shows, just after she had been awarded a third gold medal. I was attracted to her strong, positive style and bought a favourite plant of mine, a 'Jack in the pulpit' arum with scarlet berries.

Later I saw a dramatic orchid, almost crawling off the page, which was in the 'Treasures of the RHS' exhibition held in the Kew Gardens Gallery. Jonathan Cooper of Park Walk Gallery saw it too and he asked me to put him in contact with Kate Nessler. From this sprang her magnificent exhibition of orchids at his gallery in 1995 in which she has obviously reached new heights of excellence. Her thick, strappy leaves and vigorous roots form a remarkable contrast to the beautifully observed, exotic and yet delicate flowers. Her training in design serves her well in the whole orchid series.

Kate Nessler had not been idle since I first met her in 1993. She had been preoccupied with painting the prairie flowers of Arkansas (where she now lives) for a travelling exhibition thoughout the state. She only started showing botanical work relatively recently, having previously had a career as a commercial artist in Chicago. She has had solo exhibitions in New York and Illinois and is a director of the newly formed American Society of Botanical Artists. Now she must be one of the leading exponents of botanical art in the United States.

PAPHIOPEDILUM SPICERIANUM

Signed Nessler (undated)

Acquired from Park Walk Gallery, London 1995

Watercolour on paper
267 x 287 mm

JACK IN THE PULPIT

Signed Nessler (undated)

Acquired from the RHS Show 1993

Watercolour on paper
360 x 265 mm

MIYOKO OKAKURA

BORN TOKYO, JAPAN 1940

I met Miyoko Okakura when I asked her to come to a meeting of artists that I held during a brief visit to Tokyo in 1994. This attractive, dignified woman was trained at Ikenoboh Gakuen College and had a career in commercial film production at Dentsu, Sapporo, from 1960 to 1964. She started exhibiting in the Gallery Yu, Tokyo, in 1983 and has had regular shows with the Maruzen Gallery, Tokyo, since 1986. She has been published in calendars and in a medical plants brochure from 1990 to 1995. She exhibited at the Hunt Institute in 1992.

She now lives in Yokohama and arrived at the meeting laden with her portfolio. She showed me a strong and beautifully composed study of a pelargonium viewed somewhat from above, shown below.

PELARGONIUM

Signed Miyoko (undated)

Acquired from the artist 1994

Watercolour on paper 520 x 350 mm

LUCA PALERMO

BORN ROME, ITALY 1956

I visited Luca Palermo's apartment in Rome in 1995 after I had bought a painting of his in the previous year in London. I was intrigued to meet this doctor-turned-artist, who ground his own paints and worked on vellum using medieval techniques.

He welcomed me to his studio where his easel was set upright, close to an open window with the cupboard beneath stacked with pots of coloured powder and small china bowls of mixed paint. He certainly seems more like a medieval artist-scholar than a doctor now, with his flowing locks and splendid black beard, his lute propped in the corner and his library of books.

He explained to me that, although his parents were prominent doctors, he himself became disenchanted with medicine a few years after graduating with top honours from the University of Rome and decided to become a freelance flower painter, something that had fascinated him since childhood. He was also greatly influenced by an exhibition he saw at the British Museum in 1979, entitled 'Flowers in Art from East and West'.

He is particularly interested in the early techniques used for gouache, tempera and watercolour on vellum. He has studied antique books in libraries in Windsor Castle, London, Paris and Florence and he experiments with early recipes for the tempera used by the masters of the Italian Renaissance. He showed me how he pastes large sheets of vellum on to board, creating a beautifully smooth and receptive surface. He grinds his own paints and has drawers full of brightly coloured powders which he mixes daily (especially when using egg-tempera).

He has had solo exhibitions in Italy, London and New York and has been teaching botanical illustration and art techniques at the botanical garden of Rome University and also at the Accademia di Costume e Moda and the Università Popolare since 1990. He is in the Royal Collection at Windsor Castle and the Fitzwilliam Museum at Cambridge and has been published in many magazines, showing plates of several peonies in *The New Plantsman* (which is where I first saw his work). He had a successful show at the John Mitchell Gallery, London, in 1994, where I brought his *Paeonia rockii*. He showed a tulip at the 8th Hunt International Exhibition in 1995, using watercolour and tempera on vellum. I prefer his more conventional botanical paintings, although he seems to be moving towards 'tapestry' style studies, with paintings almost completely covered in leaves, sometimes with birds, which I find rather heavy-handed and lacking the subtlety that can be achieved on vellum. He is still experimenting and the medieval overtones of his work make for an interesting and distinctive Italianate style. At the moment he is the only Italian flower painter active in Italy as Marilena Pistoia stopped painting flowers.

PAEONIA ROCKII

Signed LP 1994

Acquired from John Mitchell Gallery, London 1994

Egg tempera on vellum 450 x 380 mm

Reproduced in *The New Plantsman* vol. 1:201 (1994)

JENNY PHILLIPS

BORN BOORT, VICTORIA, AUSTRALIA 1949

Jenny Phillips, although herself largely self-taught, is probably the most influential teacher in Australia, and the cluster of good botanical painters already living in Melbourne has been enlarged by students from her classes. She established the Botanical Art School of Melbourne a few years ago and has taught over 300 people during this period. In consequence her own output has recently nose-dived. However, I have seen a number of her original paintings, her portfolio and a lot of her prints at her own home in the country near Melbourne. I admire her skill with watercolour and her subtle classical style as an artist.

I own four of her paintings, two from a set of eight euphorbias that she showed at the RHS, gaining a well-deserved gold medal. I first met this fresh, attractive and intelligent woman at that exhibition and she came round to my London house to see some of my collection afterwards. A few days later she was able to come down to Hinton to see the rest. She had just been visiting galleries and libraries in Italy, England and France and this kind of study has enabled her to pass on to her students some of her own sensibility.

I met some of her class in Melbourne on a flying visit in 1995 and was very impressed with their obvious ability, but perhaps even more by the diversity of their styles – clearly Jenny Phillips had inspired each one of her students to follow an individual path.

She has had a number of one-person exhibitions in Melbourne and was in an important group show in 1994 in the Victoria Arts Centre for the Melbourne Festival, together with Celia Rosser and Margaret Stones. She has also shown at the Everard Read Gallery in Johannesburg. She has illustrated a number of books including T.R. Garnett's *Stumbling on melons* and *A gardener's potpourri* and James Haliday's *Wine atlas of Australia* She is already an established botanical artist and I feel that her influence as a teacher will have a profound effect on Australian painters not only now, but in the future.

EUPHORBIA OBESA

Signed Jenny Phillips-Goode
  1993 *Euphorbia obesa*. Hook

Acquired at the RHS Show 1993

Watercolour on paper
  225 x 255 mm

EUPHORBIA GRANDICORNIS

Signed Jenny Phillips-Goode
  1993 *Euphorbia grandicornis*.
  Goeb

Acquired at the RHS Show 1993

Watercolour on paper
  700 x 480 mm

Euphorbia   grandicornis   Goeb.

MARILENA PISTOIA

BORN MILAN, ITALY 1933

Curiously, there are very few botanical artists working today in Italy. Marilena Pistoia was an exception, with a large body of work in several big, glossy books published by Mondadori (Milan) and Calderini (Bologna). The flowers are always most beautifully arranged upon the page, often curved in soft swathes around the centre, and painted in a sensitive and yet decisive way. But somehow I did not become an enthusiast until I was shown some of the many original paintings that she had given to the Hunt Institute. The originals are more subtle, the colours better and the greens more varied. They are all very pristine and pure.

After many abortive attempts to meet her and see her studio I at last arranged to drive from Venice with some friends to visit her small house set in a garden full of English roses.

I looked around her austere studio – no artistic clutter here, only the many books she had illustrated laid out in rows – while she prepared a picnic in her immaculate home.

She had specially retrieved her flower paintings from the bank to show to me. I understood her caution when she told me that several years ago a publisher had lost 52 of her original paintings. Then she said, 'I stopped painting flowers; it was a different period of my life and it is completely finished. I only did it to make a living.' I was disturbed and rather saddened by this but she was quite adamant and now only draws futuristic globes delineated with a fine compass-operated pen. I found them intense, introspective and worrying. She spends the rest of her time as professor at the Accademia di Belle Arte di Bologna where she has taught etching since 1980.

We went back to her flower paintings and she showed me some fascinating studies of strawberries and blackberries, with the fruit magnified some tenfold. Behind the huge berry was a drawing of the flowers and leaves done at natural size. Somehow she had managed to balance each painting into a harmonious composition. They were strange and arresting pictures and had only been published (poorly) in the local newspaper.

I tried to persuade her to draw something for me or to let me buy one of her flower paintings. She refused, kindly but firmly, but she gave me this delicate painting as a consolation. The fluffy dandelion clock is so finely and lightly drawn that it is almost impossible to reproduce, but I often look at it and hope she starts painting flowers again.

DANDELION

Signed M. Pistoia (undated)

Gift from the artist 1994

Watercolour on paper 175 x 265 mm

JAGGU PRASAD

BORN JAIPUR, INDIA 1963

Jaggu Prasad has been brought up in one of India's great artistic centres. Jaipur, in Rajastan, has always been a focus for the arts and for the most brilliant artisans who produce exquisite miniatures, carved ivory and alabaster inlaid with semi-precious stones. They use traditional techniques going back for centuries. He was tutored in Indian and botanical painting by Padamshree Kripal Singh and has been learning his skills since the age of six. He showed two paintings of apples in the Hunt Institute's 7th International Exhibition in 1992 and this painting was used as the cover for the catalogue of an exhibition from Rajastan shown at the Hunt and at Wave Hill, New York, through 1994 and 1995. He is fascinated with *trompe-l'oeil* and in the traditional Indian way he is quite prepared to copy anything and has the superb skills to do so.

RED APPLES

Signed Jaggu Prasad (undated)

Acquired from the Hunt Institute 1995

Gouache on gesso on wood panel 180 x 130 mm

From a strictly botanical point of view, no other living Australian artist can rival Celia Rosser's stupendous *oeuvre* on the banksias. This unusual group of Australian plants, mainly shrubs, with their pin-cushion flowers and extraordinary cone-like fruit was first seen by Sir Joseph Banks and named after him. She has been working with the botany department of Monash University since the early 1970s, painting the plates for their monumental work *The banksias*. This monograph has been published in two mighty volumes, with a third one still in preparation. Each plate is more beautiful than the next, detailed almost beyond belief and yet so elegantly composed and placed upon the page that each painting seems the essence of that particular plant. It is a monumental work in every way as the books themselves are far too big to fit in any normal bookshelf and at the moment mine are waiting for some place of honour to be created specially for them.

I first saw the books in the library at Kew, and then later examined the original paintings when they were hung in a memorable exhibition at Kew Gardens Gallery. Celia Rosser came to London for the opening in 1993 and I met her at last.

In January 1995 we met again, on this occasion in Melbourne where I had flown for a brief one-day visit. She brought her notebooks with her field sketches and I photographed her with her preliminary work for 'my' banksia, a painting that has been finished just in time for inclusion in the exhibitions of my collection.

Celia Rosser's original training was for a Diploma in Fashion Illustration and she worked as a commercial artist before turning to botanical illustration: her first exhibition of Australian wild flower paintings was in 1965. In 1980 her delicate and beautiful drawings of mosses were published in *Mosses of South Australia* and she has been commissioned to design botanical postage stamps for Australia, the Cocos Islands and Christmas Island.

She always makes field trips when painting a particular plant to collect samples in its natural habitat. Then she roughs out her drawings on tracing paper, perhaps involving nine or ten overlays, until she is completely satisfied. After that she builds up layer upon layer of colour on transparent background washes of watercolour on paper. Often the process takes two months or more and during that time the specimen is kept refrigerated to preserve its colour. My painting of *Banksia serrata* took 16 weeks to complete and is the first major outside commission she has undertaken since the mid-1970s.

Anyone who is interested in contemporary botanical art should try to see *The banksias*; it must be one of the most outstanding works to be published this century in terms of beauty and scholarship. With it Celia Rosser takes her place among the great botanical artists of any age.

Banksia serrata was probably not the first species of banksia found by Joseph Banks when he landed in Botany Bay, Australia (then called New Holland), on 28 April 1770 but he certainly would have seen it during the second day, when he explored further inland from the seashore. *Banksia serrata* is still found near Cook's landing place at Kurnell and would have been in flower when the explorers first set foot ashore. Twenty specimens were collected and pressed in large drying books. It was amongst the first Australian species to be raised from Bank's seed in England and flowered there in a glasshouse in 1800. It grows along the coastal plain of Australia from Melbourne to Brisbane and into the Blue Mountains behind Sydney. The pale flower develops into a fruit with large seed follicles surrounded by shaggy old flowers which persist for several years.

SAW BANKSIA: *BANKSIA SERRATA*

Signed with her monogram and Celia Rosser 1995

Commissioned 1993, received 1995

Watercolour on paper 760 x 560 mm

GRAHAM RUST

BORN HERTFORDSHIRE, ENGLAND 1942

Graham Redgrave-Rust attended art school in London, at the Regent Street Polytechnic and the Central School of Arts & Crafts, and then studied at New York's National Academy of Art. He first exhibited at the Royal Academy when only 23 years old and has become internationally renowned for his murals and ceiling paintings. The most famous of these is a spectacular 'Temptation' at Ragley Hall near Stratford-upon-Avon, which took over ten years to complete. His most famous book on mural design is *The painted house* and he is presently working on a sequel called *Decorative designs* which will be published in 1996/97. He also illustrated a recent edition of *Some flowers* by Vita Sackville-West.

His watercolours and botanical paintings have been exhibited in Europe and the United States and he has had 22 solo shows in places as disparate and varied as Panama, Chicago, San Francisco and The Museum of Garden History, London. He lives in London where he has exhibited with Hazlitt, Spink and Colnaghi. He is particularly happy painting fruit and vegetables and showed a fine pumpkin at the Hunt Institute's 8th International Exhibition in 1995.

The first painting I bought was a delightful, casual sketch of narcissus and daffodils which he had donated to a gala gardening evening auction in 1994. Later I bought a most beautiful, lush and velvety iris study which shows his superb command of watercolour. He had raced down to a specialist iris nursery, Kelways, to paint it at its best.

IRIS 'SPARTAN'

Signed Graham Rust '95

Acquired from the artist 1995

Pencil, watercolour and body colour 360 x 260 mm

ROSANNE SANDERS

BORN STOKE POGES, ENGLAND 1944

Rosanne Sanders was introduced to me as the 'Apple Lady' because of her superlative studies of fruit. She now lives in cider country in Devon and has become an authority on old apple varieties. This culminated in her book *The English apple* published in 1988, which has dozens of plates showing the flowers and fruit of every imaginable type of apple (and some that have more or less vanished from cultivation).

She went to High Wycombe College of Art and started as a freelance botanical artist in 1974. She has been awarded four RHS gold medals and received the Royal Academy Miniature Award in 1985. Her work has been exhibited in Britain, and appeared in the 7th International Exhibition at the Hunt Institute in 1992.

She has been commissioned to do paintings for HM Queen Elizabeth II, HM the Queen Mother, for the RHS, the Royal National Rose Society and to design a set of wild plant stamps for Barbados.

She visited me in 1992, bringing up her portfolio from Devon. I was particularly attracted to two studies, each of three apples very simply placed upon the page, settled in position with discreet shadows. I had the pair mounted into two fine old wooden frames and they have given me immense satisfaction ever since.

DEVONSHIRE QUARRENDEN APPLE

Signed RJS (undated)

Acquired from the artist 1992

Watercolour on paper 165 x 265 mm

TOM PUTT APPLE

Signed RJS (undated)

Acquired from the artist 1992

Watercolour on paper 165 x 265 mm

MARGARET A. SAUL

BORN AUSTRALIA 1951

Margaret Saul lives in Queensland but I first saw her work in the newsletter of the Guild of Natural Science Illustrators, USA, where she had written a lively account of plant collecting and illustration in Australia.

She took a four-year course in commercial illustration in Brisbane and then launched herself on a packed schedule, working first for the Queensland Museum, then the zoology department at Queensland University and then at Queensland Herbarium, Brisbane. By 1980 she was a freelance illustrator, working on dozens of local commissions. Since 1989 she has organized and taught an annual course in botanical illustration at Brisbane Botanical Gardens. She has also painted a great number of plates for many scientific publications such as the *Flora of south-eastern Queensland*, *Flora of Australia* and *Ferns of Australia*. One of the latest books she illustrated was *Dinkum gardening: green my Australia* by T. Low.

When I commissioned her I asked her to paint me something particularly Australian. Since working in Australia in the 1970s I have always been fascinated by its unique flora and Queensland has some most unusual plants. We agreed on the 'peanut tree', *Sterculia quadrifida*, a spectacular tree which grows in her garden. This painting will also be used as the cover and frontispiece for the *Flora of Australia*, Volume 7. She collected this specimen in the Brisbane Botanical Garden, Mount Coot-tha. The black seeds are edible and taste like peanuts.

PEANUT TREE:
STERCULIA QUADRIFIDA

Signed Margaret A Saul 1995

Commissioned 1995

Watercolours with colour pencil and gouache on
Arches watercolour paper 420 x 300 mm

GILLIAN SCOTT

BORN LONDON 1933

Gillian Scott is now an Australian citizen, living in Queensland as a freelance writer and artist, and occasionally teaching botanical art and miniature painting at the well-known McGregor College Winter School at Toowoomba.

Before this she moved around a good deal, starting by going to university in Belfast to study botany and zoology. Between 1955 and 1974 she lectured at Ottawa University, Canada, and then at Flinders University, South Australia. During this period she also completed a Ph.D. in marine biology at Adelaide in 1962. From 1974 to 1978 she taught at the University of Central Queensland as a senior lecturer but retired in 1979 to pursue her present career as a writer and biological illustrator. She is a founding member of the Society of Botanical Artists.

She was awarded three medals by the RHS including a gold for Australian mistletoes in 1991 and has had several one-person exhibitions in Australia. Her work has also been exhibited at the Hunt Institute.

When I contacted her to commission a painting I particularly asked her to choose an Australian subject and we decided on a eucalyptus. There are some 450 species of eucalyptus and the vast majority of these grow in Australia – indeed *Eucalyptus* is the most characteristic genus of the Australian landscape and an important source of nectar and pollen for honey-bees. I was really delighted with the showy *Eucalyptus erythrocorys* whose flowers have a scarlet cap which drops off as they open, revealing the pompon of yellow stamens – a feature reflected in the tree's common name of 'red cap gum'. This eucalyptus is a small tree which ultimately reaches a height of about 8 metres (26 feet) and is native to western Australia. Although I once lived in Australia for a year, I still find its amazingly diverse native flora to be strange and intriguing.

RED CAP GUM:
EUCALYPTUS ERYTHROCORYS

Signed GS (undated)

Acquired from the artist 1993

Watercolour on paper 510 x 355 mm

170

PANDORA SELLARS

BORN HERTFORD, ENGLAND 1936

The very first painting I bought for my botanical collection was *Laelia tenebrosa* by Pandora Sellars, the centrepiece of a splendid exhibition mounted by the Kew Gardens Gallery in May 1990. Looking back I feel I could not have started with a more important artist or a more dramatic and complex painting.

Pandora Sellars started as a textile designer and the design element is immensely strong in her work today. She exhibited at the RHS and contributes occasionally to *Curtis's Botanical Magazine* (which became temporarily *The Kew Magazine*). She illustrated the *Flora of Jersey* (1984) and two Kew Magazine monographs – *The genus Paphiopedilum* (1987) and *The genus Arum* (1993) – and contributed to *The flowering of Kew* by Richard Mabey (1987). She painted the design for a commemorative plate and a presentation picture for HRH The Princess of Wales when the new Kew conservatory was opened by her in 1987. In 1993 she designed a set of five postage stamps depicting orchids for the British Post Office. I commis-

sioned her to do the Christmas cover for the *Illustrated London News* in 1991, a painting of Christmas roses and holly with an unusual festive red background.

Her work has been shown in all the recent books on the art of botanical illustration that have included contemporary artists and she has a devoted following of *cognoscenti* in this area.

Brinsley Burbidge wrote of her show at Kew:

'When she arrived with her first paintings for the exhibition, I was stunned by what she had produced. It was not the area of paper she had covered nor the number of paintings which impressed – for her style is detailed,

LAELIA TENEBROSA 1990

Signed Pandora Sellars 1989

Labelled: Laelia tenebrosa, Philodendron hybrid, Calatheaomata, Philodendron leichthnii, Polypodiaceae specie

Acquired at Kew Gardens Gallery 1990

Watercolour on paper 410 x 600 mm

Laelia tenebrosa was the very first purchase for my collection, catalogued as l/PS. In the beginning I bought it to support Kew Gardens Gallery but soon afterwards, becoming obsessed by collector's fever, I started to visit galleries and painters around the world. It is a rather sombre orchid, pictured against a dramatic background of tropical plants from the greenhouse tended by her husband. There is an excellent print produced from the painting. Some people have found it an almost threatening subject but I find the complexity of the leafy background absolutely fascinating and immensely satisfying.

Gloriosa rothschildiana. Pandora Sellars . 90

GLORY LILY:
GLORIOSA ROTHSCHILDIANA

Signed Pandora Sellars '90 *Gloriosa rothschildiana*

Commissioned 1990

Watercolour on paper 280 x 370 mm

I grew this glory lily through the palms and plumbago that rampaged up one of the walls of my conservatory and commissioned Pandora to paint it – the first one that she had drawn. She saw it *in situ* and then went off with a specimen to work on in her own home.

painstaking and consequently slow – but it was the sheer overwhelming quality of her work and her remarkable ability to incorporate a number of plants in a set piece which looked like a "corner of nature" which took me by surprise. These set-pieces were real botanical theatre with living subjects which seemed a million miles away from the traditional association between flower painting and what is called in English still life. Looking over the twenty or so works painted specially for this exhibition one is immediately aware of being in the presence of a consistent and superior talent in the delineation of plants: the fidelity to nature is absolute, the quality of draughtsmanship unwavering; the use of colour impeccable and the representation of texture without equal. Just as many of us first respond musically to large-scale works such as symphonies, so it is the large-scale "plant symphonies" which instantly attract and are most accessible. Chamber works often appeal later as knowledge and appreciation matures. Similarly one moves from admiration for the large complex paintings to a deep respect for the elegant but simple

174

SNAKE'S HEAD FRITILLARIES
AND COWSLIPS

Signed Pandora Sellars '91

Commissioned 1991

Watercolour on paper 280 x 320 mm

Pandora Sellars was rather uneasy at painting fritillaries and cowslips together, feeling they were not usually closely associated in the wild. But she did it to please me, as I had just started a ginkgo avenue under-planted with a mixture of both plants. The first year it was a great success, with cowslips, fritillaries and the tender yellow leaves of the ginkgo all reaching perfection at exactly the same time. After that the ginkgos stubbornly refused to produce their fresh leaves to coincide with the cowslips, and the elegant fritillary flower helmets were eaten by marauding pheasants, who neatly and literally nipped them in the bud. Today the ginkgos have at last decided to grow, the fritillaries are but a memory and the cowslips are happily seeding themselves in the most generous fashion.

Sadly not all gardening plans work, but I still have Pandora's painting to remind me of my scheme which was inspired by seeing tender fresh ginkgo leaves in Korea, fritillaries from Port Meadow in my Oxford days and abundant cowslips, such a favourite picking of my youth.

NYMPHAEA CAPENSIS

Signed Pandora Sellars '95

Commissioned 1993

Watercolour on paper 385 x 500 mm

This commission of the blue water lily took some time to materialize as Pandora only managed to paint the flowers during one summer and the leaves during another season, getting the specimens from Wyld Court Nurseries near Newbury.

The painting shows her strong sense of design, with a semi-circular backdrop of lily pads framing all stages of the graceful flower. It is painted to meticulous perfection. I find it interesting to compare it with a blue water lily, *Nymphaea ampla*, painted by Margaret Mee which has water-rippled paper and foxing from her Amazonian environment. She has also painted some leaves erect, as they so often appear standing clear of the water in calm stretches of river.

plant portraits which have formed the main body of her work for over ten years. As must be obvious from this short introduction I have the highest possible admiration for her work and I remain to be convinced that the world has ever known a botanical painter with a greater talent than

Pandora Sellars. Ehret, Redouté, Turpin, Lilian Snelling come close. Fitch, prolific, liberated and wonderful in his way approaches, and several living artists come even closer but, for me, only the brothers Bauer occupy, with her, that corner of the botanical painting world in which one can truly say that no one has ever done it better. But, were the Bauers so good at painting leaves?'

In July 1993 Pandora Sellars and her husband moved from Southampton to Herefordshire where she looks down the Wye Valley towards the Radnor Hills. It was a disruptive time for her painting as she struggled to establish her new garden and battled with the builders. Now her husband has built a new greenhouse from which she can draw inspiration. She has had time to finish a recent commission for me of a beautiful blue water lily, *Nymphaea capensis*, painted over the last two years from specimens supplied by Wyld Court Nurseries, the remarkable rainforest conservatory with several acres under glass, near Newbury, Berkshire.

VIJAY KUMAR SHARMA

BORN JAIPUR, INDIA 1962

V.K. Sharma started training in traditional Indian painting in the early 1970s when he was apprenticed to the atelier of master-painter Ramesh Sharma, who is also his uncle. After he had finished regular school for the day he would spend laborious hours, alongside many other eager children, learning the fine and demanding brush strokes used in Indian painting. He showed particular ability and is now considered one of the best of the Jaipur group of painters. There are literally hundreds of artisans there who are willing to copy postcards, pictures from newspapers or photographs. V.K. Sharma started to illustrate bonsai trees in 1987 when he was commissioned to paint them and other nature studies by an American patron.

BONSAI TREE

Unsigned and undated

Acquired from the Hunt Institute 1994

Watercolour on paper 265 x 190 mm

SIRIOL SHERLOCK

BORN NANTWICH, ENGLAND 1954

Siriol Sherlock has mastered the skill of watercolour to perfection. Her washes flow with such apparent ease that she paints straight on to the paper, and often does not use the faintest pencil guidelines. She tells me she tries to get her students to do this – but that it takes courage and experience.

As happens with so many botanical artists, she started off as a textile designer and has only ventured to show flower paintings since 1986. She has been showing regularly at the Society of Botanical Artists, the Society of Women Painters and in the Royal Institute of Painters in Watercolour, as well as at many English galleries. She has been awarded three gold medals by the RHS and showed at the Hunt Institute's 8th International Exhibition in 1995. She often paints at the Sir Harold Hillier's Gardens and Arboretum in Hampshire and has been commissioned to do plates for botanical magazines.

She had an excellent solo exhibition at Kew Gardens Gallery where I bought a pink magnolia and the white paeony 'Joseph Rock'. I later commissioned her to do me a fuchsia 'Corallina' and she has painted both leaves and flowers with great fluidity.

Now that her family have grown up, she can undertake some projects further afield. She decided to paint a series of tropical plants grown at Wyld Court Nurseries, which houses a remarkable selection of fascinating plants under several acres of glass near Newbury. It is an inspiring place and Siriol travelled from her home in Hampshire to paint orchids, passion flowers and water lilies at their peak.

I have a number of splendid plant portraits created while she was working there. Wyld Court has proved a magical place for tropical plants and a focal point for painters, gardeners and conservationists. Never have I seen such a luxuriant display in the northern hemisphere.

MAGNOLIA CAMPBELLII VAR. *MOLLICOMATA*

Signed Siriol Sherlock (undated)

Acquired from Kew Gardens Gallery 1992

Watercolour on paper 570 x 460 mm

Sirrol Sherlock

Siriol Sherlock

PAEONIA SUFFRUTICOSA
'JOSEPH ROCK'

Signed Siriol Sherlock (undated)

Acquired from Kew Gardens Gallery 1992

Watercolour on paper 620 x 460 mm

FUCHSIA 'CORALLINA'

Signed Siriol Sherlock (undated)

Commissioned 1993

Watercolour on paper 430 x 370 mm

GROUP OF LOWLAND TROPICAL PLANTS

Signed Siriol Sherlock (undated)

Acquired from the artist 1994

Watercolour on paper 650 x 480 mm

STANHOPEA TIGRINA

Signed Siriol Sherlock (undated)

Acquired from the artist 1994

Watercolour on paper 440 x 580 mm

Painted at Wyld Court Nurseries, near Newbury, England

SHEILA SIEGERMAN

BORN KAMLOOPS, BC, CANADA 1931

Sheila Siegerman has had a most varied and interesting career. She started off as a jewellery designer in Vancouver in the early 1950s, and when she was only 20 years old created a silver rose-bowl which was given to Princess Elizabeth by the city of Vancouver. After private music studies, she went on to be a freelance violinist in Toronto and Montreal, as well as working for periods as an actress and as a theatrical set designer. She was also winning awards for her jewellery, with prizes for diamond rings, and was the critics' choice for set designer of the year (1971). It was less than ten years ago that she started painting botanical watercolours and in this field she describes herself as self-taught. She has been exhibiting her work in Ontario since 1990.

She is such a lively, vivacious woman that I can well understand these many creative strands in her life. I first saw her botanical work at the Hunt Institute's 7th International Exhibition in 1992, where she showed a blockbuster orchid, fleshy, voluptuous and slightly vulgar with its red-rimmed yellow flowers displayed with vigorous roots and strong, leathery leaves. Its impact stayed with me and I eventually bought a second painting of the same plant when I met her at the RHS the next year. She was awarded a gold medal for a strong series of eight orchids, all grown in her own home and painted with great confidence. Having seen slides in advance of the show, I had tentatively chosen a different painting, but in the end I bought the *Laeliocattleya* 'Amber Glow' after dithering in an irritating fashion.

I have not regretted my final choice, and went on to use it as a cover for one of my magazines when we were illustrating an article on orchids. It is sometimes necessary to have a very decisive image for a cover. Watercolour is notoriously difficult to reproduce successfully, but this painting had the strength to print well and was received with enthusiasm. I had it framed in bold, yellow-striped sycamore as it needed something powerful and with enough impact to contain the image.

LAELIOCATTLEYA 'AMBER GLOW'

Signed Sheila Siegerman 1993

Acquired from the artist 1993

Watercolour on paper 650 x 485 mm

S. Siegerman '92

ANNIKA SILANDER-HÖKERBERG

BORN GOTHENBERG, SWEDEN 1949

I suspect that a new star is in the ascendant in the world of botanical art. Annika Silander-Hökerberg has only shown work at the RHS (where she was awarded a gold medal) and at the 8th International Exhibition at the Hunt Institute in 1995. But her paintings of tulips, lemons and irises demonstrate great confidence and quality of execution and design. She showed a wonderful painting of a euphorbia at the Hunt, which was greatly admired on the opening night with many fellow-artists crowding round to look at it with their magnifying glasses. Her mastery of dry-brush was honed at one of Kew's painting courses and she seems to catch the very essence of each subject that she paints.

She has a degree in political science and economics and, perhaps more relevantly, she studied graphic design at Konstfack, Stockholm.

I bought *Iris sibirica* from her show at the RHS and hope to see much more of her work in the future.

SIBERIAN IRIS: *IRIS SIBIRICA*

Signed A. Silander-Höckerberg 1994

Acquired from the artist 1995

Watercolour on paper 760 x 560 mm

188

ALAN SINGER AND ARTHUR SINGER

BORN NEW YORK, USA 1950

BORN MANHATTAN, NEW YORK, USA 1917–1990

It is unusual to find a painting signed by two artists but 'Cactus Wren on Saguaro' was painted by a father and son team, with Arthur Singer drawing the wren while Alan Singer painted the saguaro cactus. It was used as one of the designs for a US postage-stamp set of 'Birds and Flowers of the Fifty States' (1982) and has the most delightful impact.

Arthur Singer was one of the best-known bird painters in the United States in recent times with a huge number of exhibitions, publications and awards to his credit. He started painting birds after a period in the army in World War II when he worked on camouflage designs for tanks for the Normandy invasion. He made his living as a book illustrator producing over 20 volumes during his lifetime. His three most famous books were *Birds of the world* (1961), *Birds of North America* (1966) and *Birds of Europe* (1970). These established him amongst the most important of American bird artists. He developed a dramatic style in his paintings, somewhat at odds with some current bird illustrators who aim for almost photographic correctness. Some of his work was much influenced by the Japanese prints he collected, especially those by Hiroshige and Koson.

Like his father, Alan Singer also trained at Cooper Union, New York, and then went on to complete a Master of Fine Arts degree at Cornell University.

He was an instructor in illustration at the New York Botanical Gardens, lived in Trinidad, West Indies, for a while and is currently an assistant professor in the department of fine art, Rochester Institute of Technology, Rochester, New York.

He has written widely on the visual arts and illustrated for the *National Geographic* and many other publications and has held over a dozen solo exhibitions.

I saw this small painting in the Hunt Institute's 7th International Exhibition in 1992. About a year later I was reminded of it when I was staying in the Sonora Desert near Phoenix, Arizona. I was quietly reading when through the open window came a cactus wren, a thrush-sized bird much larger than any of the European wrens which I knew well. Clearly it was used to foraging for breakfast crumbs and it proceeded to 'vacuum' the floor before leaving in a dignified and unhurried fashion. Outside the window was a huge saguaro cactus and I saw that the wren had burrowed its nest in the mighty 'trunk' of this extraordinary plant. The saguaro stand isolated in the desert, reaching up to 9 metres (30 feet) or more and only branch after a century's growth. They impart an extraordinary quality to these desert regions.

When I wrote to Alan Singer about this painting, I was delighted to find that it was available and I now have it to remind me of that strange, austere desert landscape.

CACTUS WREN ON SAGUARO

Signed Arthur Singer, Alan Singer

Acquired from Alan Singer 1993

Gouache and watercolour on paper 175 x 120 mm

PAMELA STAGG

BORN NOTTINGHAM, ENGLAND 1949

Pamela Stagg holds joint nationality as both a British and Canadian citizen and lives in Toronto where she teaches and paints. She went to Ontario College of Art in the late 1960s and then read art history at the University of Guelph. She started botanical painting in 1987 and has since had several one-person shows in Canada, and two in London at Jonathan Cooper's Park Walk Gallery. She was awarded a gold medal by the RHS as well as their Grenfell Medal in 1992.

I first saw her work at the Hunt Institute's 7th International Exhibition in 1992. I asked to see some more of her paintings and chose a dramatic 'black' parrot tulip. Later that year she was in London and visited me to discuss her work. Somehow we got on to cats and she and my Bagpuss became friends. It is amazing how many botanical artists love cats and immediately relate to mine. Later, when she had a solo show, I bought a large, tall bearded iris and a very beautiful study of figs which have an extraordinary bloom upon them. In her next London show with Jonathan Cooper I decided to buy fruit and vegetables, this time a study, 'Miniature Aubergine and Artichoke', and five 'Fiorello' pears suspended in space.

Pamela Stagg has built up a strong reputation as a teacher and lecturer in Toronto and has illustrated numerous articles and books. She feels that many of her students are 'seriously good', so I hope to see their work sometime. I think she is very strong painting fruit and vegetables while her irises are particularly beautifully executed.

BLACK PARROT TULIP

Signed Pamela Stagg May 1991

Acquired from the artist 1992

Watercolour on paper 420 x 300 mm

Pamela Stagg
© May 1991

FOUR FIGS

Signed Pamela Stagg March 1993

Acquired from Park Walk Gallery, London 1993

Watercolour on paper 200 x 326 mm

MINIATURE AUBERGINE AND ARTICHOKE

Signed Pamela Stagg August 1993

Acquired from Park Walk Gallery, London 1994

Watercolour on paper 250 x 300 mm

MARGARET STONES

BORN VICTORIA, AUSTRALIA 1920

Margaret Stones is an Australian painter of great distinction who now lives just next door to Kew. She arrived in England in 1951, having attended art school in Australia. For many years she worked as an independent painter at Kew and from 1957 to 1981 she was the major contributing artist to *Curtis's Botanical Magazine*. She has had 17 solo exhibitions as well as group shows at the British Museum and National Gallery of Victoria, Melbourne. She has illustrated many books including the massive *The endemic flora of Tasmania* by W. Curtis (1962–77) whose six volumes contain 250 of her watercolours. She painted a collection of wild flowers from Louisiana which have been shown widely throughout the United States and the United Kingdom and which were published in *Flora of Louisiana* (1991). She has received two honorary degrees as well as the MBE. Her work has been selected for many collections ranging from the Natural History Museum in London, the Ashmolean in Oxford, the British Museum, Cornell University and the National Gallery of Victoria to the National Library of Australia.

For several years she visited Ascreavie, the Scottish home of Major George Sherriff and his wife Betty, to paint the plants growing in their garden. Sherriff and his friend Frank Ludlow were renowned plant-hunters and introduced many garden-worthy plants from the Himalaya: the garden at Ascreavie was a botanist's and painter's delight. After the death of the Sherriffs Margaret Stones' paintings were given to the Royal Botanic Garden in Edinburgh.

When I visited her home in 1993 she showed me plates of her paintings for the *Flora of Louisiana* which had just come back from the printers. I selected two paintings from her lavish portfolio, first choosing *Viburnum rhytidophyllum*, painted to show its dramatic black and scarlet berries, which I have growing in my own garden. The other was *Nerine bowdenii*.

Margaret Stones is having a major retrospective of her work in 1996 at the National Gallery of Victoria. Paintings normally curated in Louisiana and Kew will be shown alongside her work on the Tasmanian flora already held in the Queen Victoria Museum.

VIBURNUM RHYTIDOPHYLLUM

Signed Margaret Stones (undated) *Viburnum rhytidophyllum* China – RBG Kew September 2nd 1992

Acquired from the artist 1993

Watercolour on paper 482 x 370 mm

NERINE BOWDENII

Signed Margaret Stones, *Nerine bowdenii* RBG Kew 1990

Acquired from the artist 1993

Watercolour on vellum 195 x 172 mm

Nerine bowdenii RBG Kew

JESSICA TCHEREPNINE

BORN LONDON 1938

Jessica Tcherepnine now lives and works in New York, although she visits England regularly and shows in London. She describes herself as having 'no relevant education and no career' but she did start painting flowers from her family's garden in Sussex at an early age. Later, she studied drawing in Florence under Signora Simi, and learned that important facet of botanical art – intense observation.

This tall, attractive and decisive woman with her surprising shock of white hair has had solo exhibitions regularly from the early 1980s, showing in London, New York, Paris and Palm Beach, Florida. The RHS has twice awarded her their gold medal. I first met her when I bought her *Fritillaria imperialis* from Shepherd's Gallery in New York in 1991. I had noticed a large banner floating from the gallery, showing a vastly magnified drawing of the crown imperial. I wandered in and saw the original painting, which had been used as a poster for the New York Flower Show. I assumed the artist was American but was not unduly surprised to discover she was born in England, as so many botanical artists working in the United States –

Katie Lee and Katherine Manisco, for example – turn out to have British roots. She showed me an interesting portfolio of native North American plants which she hopes to publish one day.

I found that her work was at the Hunt Institute, the Natural History Museum, London, and the RHS's Lindley Library as well as in private hands.

She shared a group exhibition at Kew Gardens Gallery in 1993 where I bought a striking picture of the skunk cabbage. There is nothing sweet and flowery about this arum, which grows as squat and uncompromising clumps in damp and shady spots. But what character it has!

In fact, Jessica Tcherepnine paints more conventional flowers and fruit most beautifully and her anemone circle, used in Cara Montgomery Stephenson's book *Looking at flowers* and for the 1995 New York Flower Show, is a gem of delicacy and charm.

Recently, as one of the directors, she has been involved with setting up the new American Society of Botanical Artists in the hope of encouraging more Americans to become interested in this burgeoning field.

SKUNK CABBAGE:
SYMPLOCARPUS FOETIDUS

Signed Jessica Tcherepnine 1991

Acquired from Kew Gardens Gallery 1993

Watercolour on paper 505 x 400 mm

MICHIKO TOYOTA

Having started as a kimono designer in Yuzen, Michiko Toyota now works as a freelance botanical artist and instructor in painting at the Botanic Gardens of Toyama. She has won a variety of awards including the Superiority Prize at the International Orchid Festival, Tokyo, 1994. Since 1983 she has exhibited in a number of galleries and botanical gardens from Tokyo to Nagoya, Mito, Yokohama and the Hunt Institute in 1988. Her work has been used for posters and to illustrate several books and pamphlets.

I had asked her, together with a group of other painters, to meet me at a small reception in Tokyo in 1994. About 16 artists and their companions accepted and arrived with portfolios of work. I tried to organize the meeting in a dignified way but in the end I looked through Michiko Toyota's paintings in a corridor. She is an attractive and intelligent young woman who is in regular contact with the respected artist Yoshio Futakuchi and she offered to show me some of his work. In the meantime I was trying to choose from a splendid selection of her own paintings.

Eventually I chose a large, strongly designed painting of strelitzia, that extraordinary, dramatic and complicated 'bird of paradise' flower that so intrigues botanical artists. In addition, I bought an unusual study of oak tree seedlings that shows every stage of germination and has a big visual impact. I do not know why it is so appealing, but non-specialists always single it out as interesting and it has given me a lot of pleasure.

BIRD OF PARADISE: *STRELITZIA*

Signed Toyota (undated) Bird of Paradise Flower *Strelitzia reginae* Banks

Acquired from the artist 1994

Watercolour on paper 750 x 430 mm

SEEDLINGS OF OAK: *QUERCUS SERRATA*

Signed M. Toyota '92

Acquired from the artist 1994

Watercolour on paper 490 x 355 mm

YOKO UCHIJO

BORN TOKYO, JAPAN 1949

Yoko Uchijo has illustrated a number of books for children and is now working freelance in Tokyo. She is a good botanical painter although she has had no formal education in this field. Immediately after leaving school she was employed by a company that produced animated films, but she has recently been working at the Asahi Cultural Centre for Botanical Art, Tama, Tokyo. She is a member of the prestigious Japanese Botanical Art Association.

She exhibited in the Hunt Institute's 7th International Exhibition in 1992 and I saw more of her work when I met her in Tokyo in 1994. Yoko Uchijo uses pencil to define her watercolour and places her images very well on the paper.

SLIPPER ORCHID:
PAPHIOPEDILUM

Signed Yoko (undated)

Acquired from the artist 1993

Watercolour on pencil 335 x 240 mm

Arundhati Vartak is a lively young artist who has made painting trees one of her hallmarks. In no sense can she be described as a mainstream botanical painter, but her light-hearted compositions have all the appeal of an Indian miniature, while in fact being considerably larger. She takes all sorts of liberties with the relative proportions of different parts of the tree, but even when rejecting naturalism she somehow retains the essence and character of each one she paints.

I find her work fun.

She went to Bombay University where she gained a BA studying psychology and Marathi literature. Since 1990 she has had solo exhibitions in Bombay at The House of Soviet Culture, the Artists Centre, Jehangir Art Gallery and the Nehru Centre Art Gallery. She has made a series of delightful cards to be sold on behalf of charities such as the World Wildlife Fund (India) and the Society for the Education of the Crippled.

She has a popular following in Bombay where one critic wrote: 'The solemnity of the trunk, the languor of the branches, finds its echo in the life that flits in and around the trees.' I think what he meant was that the birds she shows in the branches are all associated with that particular tree. She showed another of her charming tree paintings, a portrait of *neem* or Indian lilac, in the Hunt Institute's 8th International Exhibition in 1995.

Anyone who has seen the cannonball tree in tropical surroundings will immediately recognize the sketch shown here. The big, brown-red flowers are scattered all over the ground and the extraordinary, huge globular fruits hang close to the trunk on short branches. It is interesting to compare this with the classic study that Margaret Mee made of the flower on her first trip to the Amazon in 1956 (plate on page 139).

CANNONBALL TREE OR KAILASPATI:
COUROUPITA GUIANENSIS

Signed by the artist (undated)

Acquired from the artist 1994

Poster colours on paper 660 x 510 mm

INDIAN CORAL TREE OR PANGAEA:
HOLOPTELIA INTEGRIFOLIA

Signed by the artist (undated)

Acquired from the artist 1994

Poster colours on paper 660 x 510 mm

ALEXANDER VIAZMENSKY

BORN LENINGRAD (ST PETERSBURG), RUSSIA 1946

Alexander Viazmensky initially trained as an electrical engineer, but he was a freelance artist from 1976 and between 1988 and 1991 he attended the Art Academy in St Petersburg. He was in the Hunt Institute's 7th International Exhibition in 1992 (which was where I first admired his work) and had held many shows before that in what was still Leningrad. He was awarded the 'Best of the Show Award' at the Millstream Arts Festival, St Joseph, Minnesota, in 1995.

He signs his letters as 'Sasha', which somehow fits his paintings better than Alexander. His fungi watercolours are exuberant: larger-than-life toadstools surrounded by all the debris of the mushroom hunt, with pine needles, dead leaves, scraps of moss, twigs and 'button' toadstools scattered over the paper. Anyone who has gone on a fungi-foray will immediately recognize the familiar mess lying in the collecting basket after a successful expedition. And yet his work is very accurate and shows every stage of the specimen's development to make for easy identification. I am particularly fond of his boletus and amanita portraits.

Sasha wrote a fascinating account of collecting fungi in Russia (in *Mushroom* 9:5–7, 1990–91) describing how the populace moves out of town before dawn to establish good strategic positions to pick their supplies as the sun rises. The competition is so intense (as indeed it is in Italy, Switzerland and France) that all sorts of decoys are arranged, and cars are driven deep into the woods during the night so that they cannot be followed to the best, most secret places. Many areas have become depleted through over-picking so he stresses how important it is to use a basket when collecting as the spores can still be scattered from the fruiting caps, escaping from cracks in the basket, during the mushroom hunt.

FLY AGARIC: *AMANITA MUSCARIA*

Signed with hieroglyphic AV in old Russian 08.90

Acquired from the artist 1992

Watercolour on paper 340 x 240 mm

BOLETUS

Signed with hieroglyphic AV in old Russian 14.09.89

Acquired from the artist 1992

Watercolour on paper 340 x 240 mm

08.90

ELLAPHIE WARD-HILHORST

BORN PRETORIA, SOUTH AFRICA; 1920–1994

Ellaphie Ward-Hilhorst was one of the nicest, most gracious people I have met while making this collection. In fact I only saw her on a few occasions when visiting Cape Town, but we corresponded quite frequently and I feel I got to know her quite well during that brief time. She died most tragically while still at the height of her powers. The sense of shock and sorrow reverberated through the scientific and artistic community.

She must certainly be placed among South Africa's greatest botanical artists and her work was recognized much further afield.

She had always drawn from an early age and her first job, during World War II, was as a map-maker for the survey department of Witwatersrand Gold Mines. In 1947 she studied watercolour for a year in the Netherlands with her uncle, Gerhardus P.L. Hilhorst, who was a well-known naturalist painter. After this she returned to South Africa and spent many years supporting herself as a freelance commercial artist in Cape Town. She retired in 1973 and almost immediately started a new career as a botanical artist. She had always loved pelargoniums and decided to paint all the known species. She collaborated with a group of botanists at Stellenbosch, producing the illustrations for three wonderful volumes on the pelargonium, involving 314 watercolours and 160 habit sketches. When I visited her studio early in 1994 she signed all three volumes for me, while I admired her more recent work.

Ellaphie Ward-Hilhorst was involved with many other distinguished publications, including the journal *Flowering plants of Africa*. *Gasterias of South Africa* was published just after her death and yet other monographs which will use her illustrations are being prepared. She had a prodigious output, producing 800 plant portraits, mostly in watercolour, during her 24 years as an active botanical artist.

She also produced some larger plant portraits for commissions (book plates are often rather small) and she showed at the Hunt Institute, the Everard Read Gallery in Johannesburg and in 'Art meets Science', a South African touring exhibition. She was awarded the Botanical Society of South Africa's Cythna Letty Gold Medal, and a gold medal at the RHS for her *Haemanthus* paintings. She is well represented in the latest edition of *The art of botanical illustration* with two plates, one of *Haemanthus*, the other of one of her famous pelargoniums, *Pelargonium tetragonum*. I bought this pelargonium painting in 1994, having run it to ground in Kew Herbarium after she told me it had been sent to London for the publication. It was just a couple of months before she died.

Her fidelity with pelargoniums was such that one research worker told me she did not need to measure a living specimen, she could get all the information she required from Ellaphie's meticulously accurate and yet beautiful plates.

The first painting I acquired was of *Crassula coccinea*, a study of a spectacular specimen that she had found herself on Table Mountain. It is an amazing picture, with every tiny flower painted to perfection and each fleshy leaf exuding succulence. Yet she has never forgotton the plant's perspective, depth and overall shape.

Later I went to her small studio in Kenilworth, Cape Town, which looked out over a courtyard filled with flowers on to a panorama of Table Mountain. She had sev-

---

CRASSULA COCCINEA

Signed E. Ward H 1993, *Crassula coccinea* – Table Mountain

Acquired from the artist 1993

Watercolour on paper 370 x 305 mm

CRASSULA COCCINEA
-TABLE MOUNTAIN

HAEMANTHUS CANALICULATUS
CYRTANTHUS LEUCANTHUS

1993

HAEMANTHUS CANALICULATUS AND CYRTANTHUS LEUCANTHUS

Signed E. Ward H 1993, *Haemanthus canaliculatus,*
   Cyrtanthus leucanthus

Acquired from the artist 1994

Watercolour on paper 380 x 280 mm

PELARGONIUM TETRAGONUM

Signed E. Ward H 1993, *Pelargonium tetragonum*

Acquired from the artist 1994

Watercolour on paper 480 x 350 mm

PELARGONIUM TETRAGONUM

eral paintings on the walls and showed me the proofs of the latest book on *Gasterias*. I decided to buy a joint study of two South African bulbs, *Haemanthus canaliculatus* and *Cyrtanthus leucanthus*, which only flower and seed after fire has swept through the veld clearing a space for their establishment. Both are very rare and, because they flower so spasmodically, have previously been very difficult to capture on paper. Dr John Rourke, a close colleague and friend of Ellaphie's at Kirstenbosch Botanical Gardens, told me she had rushed off to see them near Betty's Bay (in the Cape) before they were collected. In this way she captured the feeling of the living, growing plants. The painting was used as the cover of *Veld and Flora* magazine (December 1994).

She was a quiet, dignified and remarkable woman and is sadly missed.

TAI-LI ZHANG

BORN JIN ZHOU, CHINA 1938

I managed to contact Tai-Li Zhang through Professor Feng, who arranged for her to visit me at the huge hotel where I was staying in Beijing. She has worked as a botanical painter all her life, training at the School of Botanical Painting, Institute of Botany, Academia Sinica, Beijing, from 1958 to 1960 and then working for 35 years at the department of plant taxonomy in the Institute of Botany.

She has shown in many exhibitions in China, and in Sydney, Australia, and the Missouri Botanical Gardens in the USA. Most recently her work was represented in the African International Plant Exhibition held in the Everard Read Gallery, Johannesburg, in 1992. Over a thousand of her drawings have been reproduced in *Flora Reipublicae Popularis Sinicae*, in several of the volumes that won prizes.

She presented her portfolio rather apprehensively, perhaps intimidated by the vast, ugly suite I was occupying where I could have held a reception for at least a hundred people. We laid out her paintings on the large conference table and I was immediately impressed with the quality of some of her work. Like Professor Feng, she was reluctant to part with paintings that she had executed some years ago saying that she needed them to copy (but also, I suspect, because her eyesight is not so sharp now). Eventually I bought a beautiful classical watercolour of the blue *Paulownia elongata* which she had painted many years earlier. She was prepared to part with it because it had already been published as a botanical plate. I also bought an arresting study of *Begonia* x *argenteoguttata* painted in oil on paper. This had the 'see-through', translucent quality of some watercolours on vellum as the oil had sunk into the paper.

I asked what the large red stamp on the back was (it can be seen faintly from the front) and she explained, rather sheepishly, that it was the price tag.

Prominent in her portfolio was the painting of ginkgo that I had seen illustrated in the Hunt Catalogue of the Institute's 6th International Exhibition (1988). I have always loved ginkgo trees and planted them extensively in my garden, so I longed to have it. She would not part with it but told me that she would paint me another as she had copied it twice before. The copy duly arrived some months later, together with a charming, rather stylized painting of a yellow peony.

In retrospect I am glad I commissioned it as I have rarely seen a more attractive characterization of the ginkgo. I know she did not paint it from life, but copied her original painting, but this is a traditional aspect of Chinese art and totally acceptable in the East and I find it preferable to a print..

PAULOWNIA ELONGATA

Unsigned and undated

Acquired from the artist 1994

Watercolour on paper 285 x 210 mm

BEGONIA X ARGENTEOGUTTATA

Signed with her chop (undated)

Acquired from the artist 1994

Oil on paper 340 x 250 mm

MAIDENHAIR TREE: GINKGO BILOBA

Signed with two chops in red and two
　　Chinese characters in black (painted 1994)

Commissioned 1994

Watercolour on paper 430 x 300 mm

銀杏

APPENDIX

SADLY IT HAS PROVED IMPOSSIBLE

FOR REASONS OF SPACE TO ILLUSTRATE THE ENTIRE

SHIRLEY SHERWOOD COLLECTION IN

THE MAIN SECTION OF THE BOOK;

THE REMAINING PAINTINGS ARE SHOWN IN

COLOUR ON THE FOLLOWING PAGES.

1

5

6

2

3

4

Helleborus foetidus

7

FRANCESCA ANDERSON

See main catalogue entry for biographical details

1 *Vanda* 'Fuchs Blue'
Signed Francesca Anderson for
  Shirley Sherwood 5/92
Acquired from the artist 1992
Pen and ink 730 x 580 mm

2 *Amaryllis* (1)
Signed Francesca Anderson (undated)
Acquired from the artist 1992
Pen and ink 580 x 730 mm

3 *Amaryllis* (2)
Signed Francesca Anderson (undated)
Acquired from the artist 1992
Pen and ink 580 x 730 mm

4 *Two Arthurium*
Signed Francesca Anderson 2/92
Gift from the artist
Pen and ink 230 x 295 mm
Inscribed: To my friend and patron
  Shirley Sherwood on her 60th birthday

GILLIAN BARLOW

See main catalogue entry for biographical details

5 Yellow Parrot Tulip
Signed G. Barlow 1991
Acquired from the artist 1992
Watercolour on paper 260 x 365 mm

6 Kingcup: *Caltha palustris*
Signed G. Barlow '94
Acquired from the SBA, London 1995
Watercolour on paper 550 x 370 mm
Awarded Certificate of Botanical Merit

JENI BARLOW

Born Stevenage, England 1961
Jeni Barlow studied textile design and began a career as a knitwear designer in 1982. She turned to botanical painting in 1990 and has since held several exhibitions.

Her work was included in the Hunt Institute's 8th International Exhibition in 1995.

7 Stinking Hellebore: *Helleborus foetidus*
Signed Jeni Barlow '94
Acquired from the artist 1994
Watercolour on paper 470 x 340 mm

8

10

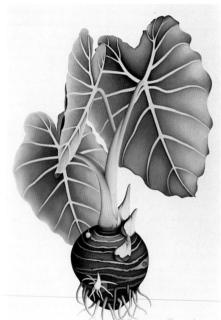

9

11

12

13

14

15

16

17

18

SUSANNAH BLAXILL

See main catalogue entry for biographical details

13 Cyclamen
Signed Susannah Blaxill (undated)
Acquired from David Ker Gallery, London 1991
Watercolour on paper 230 x 200 mm

JENNY BRASIER

See main catalogue entry for biographical details

14 Plum
Signed JMB 1995
Acquired from the SBA, London 1995
Watercolour on vellum 80 x 60 mm

15 Kumquats
Signed JMB 1995
Commissioned 1995
Watercolour on vellum 100 x 160 mm

16 *Crinum* x *powellii*
Signed JMB 1988
Acquired from Kew Gardens Gallery 1991
Pencil and watercolour 290 x 730 mm

ELIZABETH CAMERON

Born London 1915

Elizabeth Cameron trained at the Slade School of Fine Art and St John's Wood Art School in London. Marriage, children and running a business took most of her time until 1972 when she returned to painting. She has exhibited in New York, Boston, Johannesburg and at the Hunt Institute as well as in London, and has been awarded three RHS gold medals. The white gardens at Sissinghurst in Kent and Crathes Castle in Aberdeenshire inspired her to paint a series of white flowers which she published in *A book of white flowers* in 1980.

17 Dandelion
Signed EC 1986
Acquired from the artist 1993
Watercolour on vellum 320 x 240 mm

18 Purple Filbert: *Corylus maxima* 'Purpurea'
Signed EC 77
Gift from Venetia Ross Skinner 1993
Watercolour on paper 340 x 295 mm

PATRICIA DE CHAIR

Born Farnham, UK 1944

A self-taught artist, Patricia de Chair has painted and exhibited sporadically in the United Kingdom and was only able to paint seriously once her children had gone to boarding school. Her husband is an army officer and the family has moved frequently, often living in cramped accommodation which is not conducive to painting.

19 *Viola labradorica – Anemone nemorosa*
Signed P de C (undated)
Acquired from Malcolm Innes Gallery,
    London 1993
Watercolour on paper 130 x 143 mm

GILLIAN CONDY

Born Nairobi, Kenya 1952

Gillian Condy became the resident botanical artist at the National Botanical Institute in Pretoria, South Africa, in 1983. She has exhibited in South Africa and Britain since 1980, and was included in the Hunt Institute's 7th International Exhibition in 1992. She has been awarded two RHS gold medals and received the Jill Smythies Award from the Linnean Society in London in 1990. She has designed botanical postage stamps for Bophuthatswana and Botswana, and her work has been reproduced in a number of publications; notably she painted more than 170 illustrations for the journal *Flowering Plants of Africa*.

20 *Erythrina caffra*
Signed G. Condy 1990
Acquired from the artist 1992
Watercolour on paper 260 x 250 mm

JILL COOMBS

Born England 1935

Jill Coombs studied ceramics and textile design at West Sussex College of Art. She drew illustrations for various Floras for Kew and was Orchid Artist for the RHS in the mid-1980s. Her watercolours have appeared in books and journals and she designed the 1990 RHS Chelsea Plate. She has been awarded three gold medals by the RHS.

21 Gooseberry: *Ribes grossularia*
Signed Jill Coombs '93
Acquired from Kew Gardens Gallery 1994
Watercolour on paper 250 x 190 mm

19

20

21

22

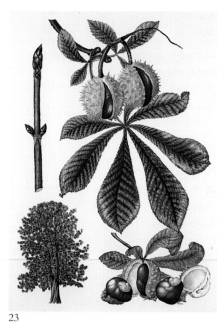

23

PATRICIA DALE

Born London 1930

Patricia Dale studied at the Putney School of Art and has been a freelance illustrator since 1972. She has shown her work in the United Kindom, the USA and Germany. A frequent exhibitor at the RHS, Westminster shows, she designed the 1995 RHS Chelsea Plate. Her work has been used on many greetings cards and calendars.

22 Scarborough Lily: *Cyrtanthus elatus*
  (Vallota speciosa)
Signed Patricia Dale (undated)
Acquired from the RHS Show 1993
Watercolour on paper 710 x 470 mm

PAULINE M. DEAN

See main catalogue entry for biographical details

23 Horse Chestnut
Signed P.M. Dean (undated)
Acquired from Kew Gardens Gallery 1991
Watercolour on paper 460 x 340 mm

24 Earth Star: *Geastrum triplex*
Signed P.M. Dean (undated)
Acquired from the RHS Show 1993
Watercolour on paper 127 x 200 mm

ETIENNE DEMONTE

See main catalogue entry for biographical details

25 *Bauhinia* and Humming-bird
Signed Etienne Demonte 1994
Acquired from the artist 1994
Gouache and watercolour on paper
  650 x 480 mm

LUDMYLA DEMONTE

Born Petrópolis, Brazil 1966

Ludmyla is the daughter of Rosália Demonte and is carrying on the family tradition of painting subjects from nature. Her paintings have been exhibited in Brazil and the United States, including in the Hunt Institute's 7th International Exhibition in 1992. She is well known for her

24

25

paintings of jaguars and other cats of the Brazilian rainforest.

26 Passion Flower and Humming-bird
Signed Ludmyla Demonte 1991
Acquired from the Hunt Institute 1992
Gouache on paper 500 x 350 mm

ROSALIA DEMONTE

See main catalogue entry for biographical details

27 *Aristolochia gigantea*
Signed Rosalia Demonte 1985
Acquired from the artist 1992
Watercolour and gouache on paper
  660 x 480 mm

26

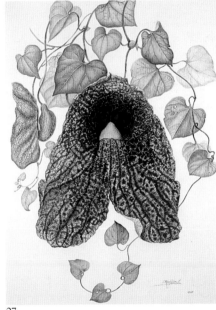

27

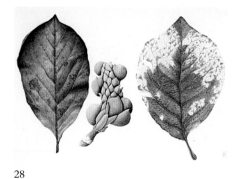

28

29

31

32

30

33

BRIGID EDWARDS

See main catalogue entry for biographical details

28 Magnolia Leaves and Fruit
Signed BE 87
Acquired from the artist 1992
Watercolour over pencil on vellum 180 x 250 mm

29 Two Red Onions
Signed Brigid Edwards 1992
Commissioned 1992
Watercolour over pencil on vellum 280 x 220 mm

30 Primulas
Signed Brigid Edwards (undated)
Acquired from Kew Gardens Gallery 1994
Watercolour over pencil on paper 450 x 330 mm
Plate XIX from *Primula* by J. Richards

31 Hydrangea
Signed Brigid Edwards 1993
Acquired from Kew Gardens Gallery 1994
Watercolour over pencil on vellum 330 x 275 mm

32 Red Onion
Signed Brigid Edwards 1995
Acquired from Thomas Gibson Fine Arts,
    London 1995
Watercolour over pencil on vellum 660 x 457 mm

33 Squash
Signed Brigid Edwards 1995
Acquired from Thomas Gibson Fine Arts,
    London 1995
Watercolour over pencil on vellum 382 x 305 mm

MARGARET FARR

Born Macon, Georgia, USA 1951
Margaret Farr took a BA in art history at the
University of North Carolina in 1974 and then
studied commercial art in Virginia. Her paintings
have been exhibited in Virginia and Colorado, as
well as in the Hunt Institute's 7th International
Exhibition in 1992.

34 Tulip Bouquet
Signed Margaret Farr 1992
Acquired from the artist 1992
Watercolour on paper 660 x 490 mm

34

35

ANN FARRER

See main catalogue entry for biographical details

35 Banana: *Musa* sp.

Signed Ann Farrer 1991

Commissioned 1991

Watercolour on paper 630 x 460 mm

Flowers of Endangered Rainforests

36 *Paphiopedilum parishii*

Signed Ann Farrer 1990

Acquired from the artist 1991

Watercolour on paper 350 x 250 mm

37 *Passiflora coccinea*

Signed Ann Farrer 1990

Acquired from the artist 1991

Watercolour on paper 340 x 260 mm

38 *Thunbergia grandiflora*

Signed Ann Farrer 1990

Acquired from the artist 1991

Watercolour on paper 340 x 260 mm

39 *Allamanda cathartica*

Signed Ann Farrer 1990

Acquired from the artist 1991

Watercolour on paper 340 x 260 mm

40 *Phalaenopsis aphrodite*

Signed Ann Farrer 1990

Acquired from the artist 1991

Watercolour on paper 355 x 270 mm

38

36

39

37

40

ANN FARRER *continued*

41 *Juncus maritimus*
Signed Ann Farrer 1981/3
Acquired from Kew Gardens Gallery 1994
Watercolour on paper 240 x 155 mm

42 *Clematis* 'Miss Bateman'
Signed Ann Farrer 92/94
Commissioned 1994
Watercolour on paper 600 x 430 mm

43 Swamp Cypress: *Taxodium distichum*
Signed Ann Farrer Sept. 1995
Commissioned 1993, received 1995
Watercolour on paper 490 x 690 mm

JINYONG FENG

See main catalogue entry for biographical details

44 *Camellia chrysantha*
Signed with his name and in Chinese characters
Acquired from the artist 1994
Watercolour and gouache on
    Winsor & Newton paper 410 x 310 mm

45 *Camellia vietnamensis*
Signed Jinyong Feng plus his Chinese chop,
    Camellia vietnamensis Hu et Huang
Acquired from the artist 1994
Watercolour on paper 410 x 310 mm

43

41

44

42

45

MARY GRIERSON

See main catalogue entry for biographical details

46 *Allium* Collection
Signed Mary Grierson '87
Acquired from Spink, London 1990
Watercolour on paper 530 x 340 mm

47 Passion Flower
Signed M G (undated)
Acquired from Spink, London 1990
Watercolour on paper 230 x 130 mm

48 *Epigeneium coelogyne*
Signed Mary Grierson (undated)
Acquired from Kew Gardens Gallery 1993
Watercolour on paper 400 x 290 mm

NOEL GRUNWALDT

Born Carmel, California, USA 1964
Noel Grunwaldt now lives in Albany, New York, and works as a freelance illustrator. She finished her Masters degree in studio art in 1989 and since then has shown in a variety of group exhibitions, some of them connected with the Guild of Natural Science Illustrators. She has also shown in galleries in New York City, Albany and Chicago. She produces very strong, powerful studies of fruit and it will be interesting to see how she develops in the future.

49 Two Pears
Signed Grunwaldt (undated)
Acquired from the artist 1993
Watercolour on paper 210 x 190 mm

CORAL GUEST

See main catalogue entry for biographical details

50 Rose 'Alba Maxima'
Signed Coral Guest '94
Acquired from the artist 1994
Watercolour on paper 460 x 370 mm

46

48

47

49

50

51

54

55

52

56

53

JOSEPHINE HAGUE

See main catalogue entry for biographical details

51 Hips and Haws
Unsigned and undated
Acquired from Kew Gardens Gallery 1990
Watercolour on paper 355 x 260 mm

52 Cornfield Plants
Signed Josephine Hague (undated)
Acquired from Kew Gardens Gallery 1990
Watercolour on paper 210 x 150 mm

53, **54** Two studies of *Clematis* 'Vyvyan Pennell'
Signed Josephine Hague (undated)
Commissioned 1991
Watercolour on paper 305 x 240 mm

CHRISTINE HART-DAVIES

See main catalogue entry for biographical details

55 Australian Pitcher Plant: *Cephalotus follicularis*
Signed Christine Hart-Davies (undated)
Acquired from Kew Gardens Gallery 1994
Watercolour on paper 230 x 240 mm

HELEN HAYWOOD

See main catalogue entry for biographical details

56 Lords and Ladies
Signed H.A. Haywood (undated)
Acquired at the Museum of Garden History,
    London 1994
Watercolour on vellum 223 x 173 mm

57 Kingcups
Signed H.A. Haywood (undated)
Acquired at the Museum of Garden History,
    London 1994
Watercolour on vellum 222 x 180 mm

HELGA HISLOP

Born London 1941

Helga Hislop went to school in Sydney, Australia, then trained at the Cardiff College of Art and the Central School of Arts and Crafts as a graphic designer. She changed to flower painting in 1978, often working on a honey-coloured, crinkled vellum. She is known for her meticulous, detailed and very restrained bunches of spring and summer flowers which have been bought by many private collectors. She has shown her work at the Mall Galleries, London, Guildford House and the Linnean Society in London and is a founder member of the Society of Botanical Artists.

58 Winter into Spring Carousel
Signed Helga Hislop '90
Acquired from the artist 1994
Watercolour on paper 250 x 340 mm

59 Rose Hips
Signed Helga Hislop (undated)
Acquired from the artist 1994
Watercolour on paper 250 x 340 mm

NICOLE HORNBY

Born London; 1908–1988

'Nic' Hornby studied at art schools in London and Florence and exhibited her work at the Trafford Gallery, London, and the Bodley Gallery, New York, in the 1950s and 1960s. She had a large exhibition at Partridge, London, in 1976. She painted charming watercolours of flowers grown in the superb garden which she and her husband, Michael, created at Pusey House, Oxfordshire.

60 Cyclamen
Signed Nicole Hornby '82
Gift from Sir Simon Hornby 1994
Watercolour on paper 215 x 215 mm

J.P. IRANI

Born Devlavi, India 1938

J.P. Irani trained as a commercial artist and spent 38 years working in advertising agencies. His paintings were exhibited in Bombay in 1988 and 1989 and his illustrations have been used in several books on birds. He has designed postage stamps for India and Bhutan.

61 *Vanda teres*
Signed J.P. Irani (undated)
Acquired from the artist 1994
Watercolour on paper 300 x 370 mm

62 Jacob's Coat: *Acalypha wilkesiana*
Signed J.P. Irani '89
Gift from the artist 1994
Watercolour on paper 365 x 250 mm

57

58

59

60

61

62

MARILYN JONES

Born England 1947

Marilyn Jones graduated from the Camberwell School of Art in London after working for 11 years in the botany department of the Natural History Museum, London. She has exhibited her watercolours in North Wales and at Ness Gardens (University of Liverpool) and has received a silver gilt medal from the RHS.

63 *Rhododendron augustinii*
Signed M.R. Jones 1993
Acquired from the RHS Show 1993
Watercolour on paper 390 x 310 mm

ANNETTE DE JONQUIERES

See main catalogue entry for biographical details

64 *Neoregelia grande*
Signed Annette de Jonquières Bangkok 1989
Gift from the artist 1991
Watercolour on paper 600 x 460 mm

JENNY JOWETT

Born Bromley, England 1936

A Diploma in Dairy Husbandry and Horticulture led Jenny Jowett on to a three-year course in lithography and printing. She has been a freelance artist since the mid-1970s, exhibiting many times in the United Kingdom as well as in the Hunt Institute's 6th International Exhibition in 1988 and at the Everard Read Gallery in Johannesburg. She teaches painting courses both in Britain and abroad. She has been awarded two RHS gold medals and designed the 1992 RHS Chelsea Plate. Her work has been reproduced on greeting cards and she produced botanical lithographs for Christies Contemporary Art in 1978 and 1979.

65 Lenten Rose: *Helleborus orientalis*
Signed Jenny Jowett '92
Acquired from the artist 1993
Watercolour on paper 480 x 370 mm

YOKO KAKUTA

Born Talien, China 1939

Japanese artist Yoko Kakuta followed a career in teaching after studying at Ochanomizu University, Tokyo. She then became a student of the botanical artist Ohta Yoai and began to exhibit her work in the 1980s, when she also became an

63

65

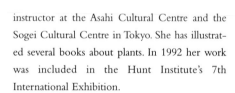

64

66

67

instructor at the Asahi Cultural Centre and the Sogei Cultural Centre in Tokyo. She has illustrated several books about plants. In 1992 her work was included in the Hunt Institute's 7th International Exhibition.

66 *Camellia japonica*
Signed Y. Kakuta (undated)
Acquired from the artist 1993
Watercolour on paper 430 x 340 mm

67 *Rosa hirtula*
Signed Y. Kakuta (undated)
Acquired from the artist 1994
Watercolour on paper 420 x 330 mm

MARTHA G. KEMP

Born Houston, Texas, USA 1944

Martha Kemp studied interior design and sociology in California in the 1960s and returned to college from 1991 to 1993 to study botanical drawing although she had been a freelance artist since 1975. She has exhibited in California, and at the RHS where she was awarded a silver gilt medal in 1993 and a gold in 1995.

68 *Fragaria* x *Potentilla* 'Pink Panda'
Signed M.G. Kemp '93
Acquired from the RHS Show 1993
Watercolour on paper 275 x 380 mm

68

PATRICIA KESSLER

Born Michigan, USA 1948

Patricia Kessler received a Bachelor of Fine Arts degree from Wayne State University and has studied under a number of recognized artists. Her work has been exhibited widely in the United States, including in the Hunt Institute's 7th International Exhbition in 1992.

69 *Phalaenopsis*
Signed Kessler 3/92
Acquired from the artist 1992
Watercolour on paper 700 x 500 mm

69

SHARON MORRIS KINCHELOE

Born Winston-Salem, North Carolina, USA 1952
After studying art at Old Dominion University and Tidewater Community College in Virginia, Sharon Morris Kincheloe spent some time as a commercial artist. She then turned freelance and for the last 14 years has made etchings and coloured-pencil drawings of the native flowers of Virginia where she now lives, as well as portraying plants from other areas of North America. She has had several exhibitions in the United States, and her work was shown in the Hunt Institute's 7th International Exhibition in 1992.

70 Showy Lady's Slipper: *Cypripidium reginae*
Signed S. Morris Kincheloe '87
Acquired from the artist 1992
Watercolour on paper 470 x 225 mm

70

CHRISTABEL KING

See main catalogue entry for biographical details

71 *Echinopsis tubiflora*
Signed C.F. King
Labelled: Echinopsis tubiflora Cult C.F. King
    26/6/93
Commissioned 1994
Watercolour on paper 670 x 520 mm

71

MARIKO KOJIMA

See main catalogue entry for biographical details

72 Roses
Signed Mari (undated)
Acquired from the artist 1994
Watercolour on paper 430 x 330 mm

72

73

75

74

76

77

VIET MARTIN KUNZ

See main catalogue entry for biographical details

73 Brussels Sprouts 1991
Signed V.M. Kunz (undated)
Acquired from the artist 1992
Watercolour on paper 480 x 345 mm

JOANNA ASQUITH LANGHORNE

See main catalogue entry for biographical details

74 Slipper Orchid: *Paphiopedilum*
Signed Joanna A. Langhorne (undated)
Acquired from Kew Gardens Gallery 1993
Watercolour on paper 230 x 155 mm

KATIE LEE

See main catalogue entry for biographical details

75 Pink Passion Flower: *Passiflora mollissima*
Orange-throated Sun Angel Humming-bird:
    Heliangelus mavors
Signed KT 1993
Acquired from the artist 1993
Gouache on Stonehenge Print 560 x 330 mm

PETR LISKA

See main catalogue entry for biographical details

76 Plum: *Prunus domestica*
Signed Liška '93
Acquired from the artist 1994
Acrylic on paper 210 x 150 mm

ELIZABETH JANE LLOYD

Born London; 1928 – 1995
A godchild of the architect Sir Edwin Lutyens,
Elizabeth Jane Lloyd studied at the Chelsea
School of Art and later at the Royal College of Art
in London. She exhibited widely after 1953 and
her paintings were accepted for the Royal
Academy Summer Exhibition almost continuous-
ly until her death.

    She taught in various art schools in the United
Kingdom and the United States as well as in her
own studio in Chiswick, London.

77 Passion Flower
Signed with her initials (undated)
Acquired from Kew Gardens Gallery 1991
Watercolour on paper 740 x 540 mm

KATHERINE MANISCO

See main catalogue entry for biographical details

78 Sunflower: *Helianthus annuus*
Signed K. Manisco '92
Acquired at the Horticultural Society of
New York 1992
Watercolour on paper 350 x 325 mm

79 Asparagus
Signed K. Manisco '95
Gift from the artist 1995
Watercolour on paper 470 x 520 mm

ALISTER MATHEWS

Born Prestwich, England 1939
After graduating from the University of Wales
Alister Mathews taught in secondary education
for four years before becoming a freelance artist.
She began to exhibit her watercolours in the late
1970s. Her work was included in the Hunt
Institute's 8th International Exhibition in 1995.

80 Lenten Rose: *Helleborus orientalis*
Signed Alister Mathews (undated)
Acquired from Malcolm Innes Gallery,
London 1992
Watercolour on paper 460 x 320 mm

81 Redcurrants
Signed Alister Mathews (undated)
Acquired from the SBA, London 1995
Watercolour on paper 132 x 95 mm

78

80

79

81

82

83

84

85

86

87

MARGARET MEE

See main catalogue entry for biographical details

82 *Aristolochia eriantha*
Signed Margaret Mee (undated)
Aristolochia eriantha Mart. Zucc. Instituto de
  Botanica, S. Paulo, March '59
Acquired from Greville Mee, Brazil 1990
Watercolour on paper 640 x 470 mm

83 *Sophronites grandiflora*
Signed Margaret Mee (undated)
  Sophronites grandiflora
Acquired from Tryon Gallery, London 1992
Watercolour on paper 560 x 390 mm

84 *Nidularium seidelii*
Signed Margaret Mee (undated)
Acquired from Greville Mee, Brazil 1993
Watercolour on paper 640 x 470 mm

KATE NESSLER

See main catalogue entry for biographical details

85 Clamshell Orchid: *Encyclia cochleata*
Signed Nessler (undated)
Acquired from Park Walk Gallery, London 1995
Watercolour on paper 845 x 685 mm

GEORGE OLSON

Born Lake City, Minnesota, USA 1936
George Olson has been professor of art at The
College of Wooster in Ohio since 1963 and has
had many exhibitions of his prints and watercolours both in the United States and the United
Kingdom since 1983. He is perhaps best known
for his paintings of native American prairie plants.

86 Willow-leaf Sunflower: *Helianthus salicifolius*
Signed Olson (undated)
Acquired from the artist 1993
Watercolour on paper 590 x 395 mm

87 Common Milkweed: *Asclepias syriaca*
Signed Olson (undated)
Acquired from the artist 1993
Watercolour on paper 555 x 445 mm

RONALDO LUIS PANGELLA

Born São Paolo, Brazil 1956

Ronaldo Luis Pangella has been exhibiting his botanical watercolours in Brazil since 1993 and his work was included in the Hunt Institute's 8th International Exhibition in 1995.

He combines mountaineering and painting in a special series of orchid studies on the Sugar Loaf Mountain, Rio de Janeiro.

88 *Zygopetalum mackayi*
Signed Pangella '95 Zygopetalum mackayi
    Hook, Paô de Acúcar, Rio de Janeiro
Gift from the artist 1995
Watercolour on paper 700 x 500 mm

JENNY PHILLIPS

See main catalogue entry for biographical details

89 Magnolia
Unsigned and undated
Acquired from the artist 1995
Watercolour on paper 400 x 480 mm

90 Figs and Currants
Signed Jenny K. Phillips Sept '95
Gift from the artist 1995
Watercolour on paper 110 x 125 mm

KATHY PICKLES

Born London 1953

Kathy Pickles obtained a degree in the history of art from the University of Sussex in 1977 and for the next seven years did secretarial work in London and in Orkney, Scotland, where she now lives. She began to show her paintings in galleries in Orkney in 1988 and has exhibited further afield since 1991: the Hunt Institute included one of her works in their 8th International Exhibition in 1995. The RHS has awarded her four gold medals and she has been commissioned to design the RHS Chelsea Plate for 1997.

91 Auricula: *Primula auricula*
Signed Kathy Pickles '93
Acquired from the artist 1993
Watercolour on paper 160 x 147 mm

88

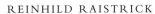

89

REINHILD RAISTRICK

Born Tanzania 1940

Reinhild Raistrick trained in England as an art teacher and taught both there and in Tanzania. She has had several exhibitions in England, where she now lives, and has been awarded two gold medals by the RHS.

92 *Dactylorhiza incarnata* and *Equisetum palustre*
Signed Reinhild Raistrick 25.5.94
Early Marsh Orchid (Dactylorhiza incarnata),
    Marsh Horsetail (Equisetum palustre) Water
    Meadows, Barton Mills, Suffolk
Acquired at the RHS Show 1994
Watercolour on paper 360 x 250 mm

90

91

92

233

KAY REES-DAVIES

Born Brighton, England 1936

An education in art, music and drama led Kay Rees-Davies to a career in teaching and lecturing, from 1956 to 1976. In 1987 she became a freelance botanical artist and has recently taught courses on botanical art at Ness Gardens (University of Liverpool). Her paintings have been exhibited in the United Kingdom and in the Hunt Institute's 8th International Exhibition in 1995, and have been reproduced as greeting cards and calendars.

93 Sulphur Heart Ivy
Signed Kay Rees-Davies Nov. 1993
Acquired at the RHS Show 1993
Watercolour on paper 405 x 330 mm

93

GRAHAM RUST

See main catalogue entry for biographical details

94 Daffodils and Narcissus
Signed Graham Rust 1994
Acquired at a gala charity ball 1994
Watercolour on paper 240 x 165 mm

MARGARET A. SAUL

See main catalogue entry for biographical details

95 *Dendrobium kingianum*
Signed Margaret A. Saul 1995
   Dendrobium kingianum
Commissioned 1995
Coloured pencil on drafting film 230 x 155 mm

95

SARA ANNE SCHOFIELD

Born Twickenham, England 1937

Sara Anne Schofield studied at Twickenham College of Art, worked at Kew and has had many exhibitions in London and elsewhere in the United Kingdom. She holds two gold medals from the RHS and is a founder member of the Society of Botanical Artists. Her work is in the Hunt Institute's collection.

96 Poppies, Day Lilies and *Crocosmia*
Signed Sara Anne Schofield (undated)
Acquired at Kew Botanic Gardens Auction –
   Conservation International 1993
Watercolour on paper 600 x 430 mm

96

97

98

99

100

101

102

103

JENEVORA SEARIGHT

Born England 1936

Jenevora Searight studied in Paris and later worked on picture restoration in London. She is self-employed and in the last ten years has concentrated on natural history subjects.

She travels widely in Brazil where she researches and sketches habitats, animals, birds and plants and has done illustrations for future books on bromeliads and macaws.

97 Bombax
Signed J. Searight (undated)
Eriotheca macrophylla (Schum.) A. Robyns
    Imbiruçu
Acquired from the artist 1995
Watercolour on paper 560 x 440 mm

PANDORA SELLARS

See main catalogue entry for biographical details

98 Christmas Rose and Holly
Signed Pandora Sellars '91
Commissioned for cover of
    Illustrated London News Christmas 1991
Watercolour on paper 192 x 170 mm

SIRIOL SHERLOCK

See main catalogue entry for biographical details

99 *Paphiopedilum lawrenceanum*
Signed Siriol Sherlock (undated)
Acquired from the artist 1994
Watercolour on paper 700 x 400 mm

100 Banana Passion Flower: *Passiflora mollissima*
Signed Siriol Sherlock (undated)
Acquired from the RHS Show 1995
Watercolour on paper 470 x 355 mm

PAMELA STAGG

See main catalogue entry for biographical details

101 Tall Bearded Iris 'Going My Way'
Signed Pamela Stagg June 1992
Acquired from Park Walk Gallery, London 1993
Watercolour on paper 650 x 440 mm

102 Five Fiorello Pears
Signed Pamela Stagg February 1994
Acquired from Park Walk Gallery, London 1994
Watercolour on paper 280 x 510 mm

PENNY STENNING

Born England 1940

Penny Stenning has had no formal training in botanical illustration apart from attending short courses held at the Chelsea Physic Garden, where she has also exhibited her paintings. She began to paint seriously some ten years ago.

103 *Gloxinia*
Signed Stenning (undated)
Acquired at the SBA, London 1995
Watercolour on paper 285 x 420 mm

ANN SWAN

Born England 1949

Ann Swan qualified in textile design in the 1960s at the Manchester College of Art and Design and worked for many years in advertising and industry. She began to exhibit her drawings in 1990 and has since shown her work widely in England. She has received two gold medals from the RHS and was awarded a silver medal at the 14th World Orchid Conference. Most of her very detailed drawings are in pencil, but she sometimes uses conte pencil or pastel to apply small areas of colour. She showed a superb drawing in the Hunt Institute's 8th International Exhibition in 1995.

104 Mangosteen: *Garcinia mangostana*
Signed Ann Swan, *Garcinia mangostana* (undated)
Acquired from Kew Gardens Gallery 1994
Conte pencil and pencil on paper 350 x 330 mm

KAZUTO TAKAHASHI

Born Changchun, China 1951

Japanese artist Kazuto Takahashi was educated at the Art Academy of Musashino and has worked for the Showa Rubber Chemical Industry Co. since 1985. He works mainly in pencil and watercolour. He has received a number of awards and three of his paintings are in the National Museum of Science, Tsukuba, Ibaragi prefecture, Japan.

105 Sow Thistle: *Sonchus oleraceus*
Unsigned and undated
Acquired from the artist 1992
Watercolour on paper 490 x 720 mm

104

105

106

107

MARY TARRAWAY

Born Wimborne, England 1928

A degree in botany led Margaret Tarraway to a career as a biology teacher. In 1991, after her retirement, she began to exhibit her botanical paintings and has continued to show her work in the United Kingdom.

She was included in the Hunt Institute's 8th International Exhibition in 1995.

106 Elderberries: *Sambucus nigra*, and Hops:
    Humulus lupulus
Signed Mary Tarraway (undated)
Acquired from the artist 1994
Watercolour on paper 480 x 350 mm

JESSICA TCHEREPNINE

See main catalogue entry for biographical details

107 Crown Imperial: *Fritillaria imperialis*
Signed Jessica Tcherepnine 1990
Acquired from Shepherd's Gallery,
    New York 1991
Watercolour on paper 510 x 375 mm

YOKO UCHIJO

See main catalogue entry for biographical details

108 *Cyclamen persicum*
Signed Yoko *Cyclamen persicum* Mill (undated)
Acquired from the artist 1993
Watercolour on paper 400 x 330 mm

109 Japanese Stewartia: *Stewartia pseudo-camellia*
Signed Yoko *Stewartia pseudo-camellia* (undated)
Acquired from the artist 1994
Watercolour on paper 250 x 350 mm

CAROL WOODIN

Born Salamanca, New York, USA 1956
Carol Woodin is self-taught and has been a free-lance artist since 1990. Her paintings have been shown in both the United States and the United Kingdom and she was included in the Hunt Institute's 8th International Exhibition in 1995. She is currently painting the plates for a book on the orchid genus *Phragmipedium*, which will be published by Kew.

110 Showy Lady's Slipper: *Cypripedium reginae*
Signed Carol Woodin '92 *Cypripedium reginae*
Acquired from the artist 1994
Watercolour on paper 550 x 420 mm

ELEANOR B. WUNDERLICH

Born New York, USA 1925
Eleanor Wunderlich trained in design and water-colour painting and has been an instructor at the New York Botanical Garden since 1984. She has exhibited widely since 1983 and her work was shown in the Hunt Institute's 8th International Exhibition in 1995. Her book *Botanical illustration watercolour technique* is a 'how to do it' manual.

111 Pink Flowering Dogwood: *Cornus florida*
   var. *rubra*
Signed Eleanor B. Wunderlich 1993,
   Cornus florida v. rubra, Pink flowering dogwood
Acquired from the artist 1993
Watercolour on paper 350 x 440 mm

108

109

110

111

112

TAI-LI ZHANG

See main catalogue entry for biographical details

112 *Paeonia delavayi* var. *lutea*
Signed with two red chops and three Chinese
   characters in black
Acquired from the artist 1994 (painted 1994)
Watercolour on paper 425 x 320 mm

GENERAL BOOKS

Blunt, W. & Stearn, W.T. 1950. *The art of botanical illustration*. Collins, London.

—1994. *The art of botanical illustration* (2nd edn). Antique Collectors' Club, Suffolk in association with Royal Botanic Gardens, Kew.

de Bray, L. 1989. *The art of botanical illustration*. Christopher Helm, Bromley & Wellfleet Press, NJ.

Elliott, B. 1994. *Treasures of the Royal Horticultural Society*. Herbert Press in association with the RHS, London.

Foshay, E. 1984. *Reflections of nature: flowers in American art*. Alfred A. Knopf, NY in association with the Whitney Museum of American Art.

Gooding, J. 1991. *Wildflowers in art: artists impressions of western Australian wildflowers 1699–1991*. Art Gallery of Western Australia, Perth.

Hulton, P. & Smith, L. 1979. *Flowers in art from East and West*. British Museum Publications, London.

Rix, M. 1981. *The art of the botanist*. Lutterworth Press, Guildford & London.

Saunders, G. 1995. *Picturing plants*. Zwemmer in association with the V & A Museum, London.

Stearn, W.T. 1990. *Flower artists of Kew*. Herbert Press, London in association with the Royal Botanic Gardens, Kew. American edition published as *Botanical masters, plant portraits by contemporary artists* by Prentice Hall, NY (1990).

Stephenson, C.M. 1994. *Looking at flowers*. K.P. International Inc., West Palm Beach, FL.

Sydney, C. 1986. *Flower painting*. Phaidon, Oxford.

Trapnell, D. 1991. *Nature in art*. David & Charles, Newton Abbot and London.

Catalogues of the International Exhibitions held at the Hunt Institute for Botanical Documentation, Carnegie Mellon University, Pittsburgh, Pennsylvania, USA are an important source of information on contemporary botanical artists. There are now eight, covering 30 years of exhibitions and issued from 1964 to 1995.

BOOKS ILLUSTRATED BY SPECIFIC ARTISTS

The artists are listed alphabetically by surname. Only books which have been illustrated wholly or partly by the artist concerned are listed. Work which has appeared in journals, on dust jackets, calendars or greeting cards etc. is not mentioned here.

Anderson, Fay

Goldblatt, P. 1986. *The Moraeas of southern Africa*. National Botanic Gardens, Kirstenbosch in association with Missouri Botanical Garden.

—1989. *The genus Watsonia*. National Botanic Gardens, Kirstenbosch.

—1993. *The woody Iridaceae*. Timber Press, OR in association with Missouri Botanical Garden and National Botanical Institute, Kirstenbosch.

Rourke, J.P. 1981. *The Proteas of southern Africa*. Purnell, Cape Town. (2nd edn, 1982, Centaur, Johannesburg.)

Blackadder, Elizabeth

Bumpus, J. 1988. *Elizabeth Blackadder*. Phaidon, Oxford.

Kellaway, D. 1994. *Favourite flowers*. Pavilion, London.

Blamey, Marjorie

Blamey, M. 1984. *Learn to paint flowers in watercolour*. Collins, London.

—& Grey-Wilson, C. 1989. *The illustrated flora of Britain and northern Europe*. Hodder & Stoughton, Great Britain.

—1993. *Mediterranean wild flowers*. HarperCollins, Great Britain.

Fitter, R.S. & Fitter, A. 1974. *The wild flowers of Britain and northern Europe*. Collins, London.

Gibson, M. 1973. *Shrub roses for every garden*. Collins, London.

Grey-Wilson, C. & Blamey, M. 1979. *The alpine flowers of Britain and Europe*. Collins, London.

Lloyd, C. 1977. *Clematis*. Collins, London.

Mabey, R. 1977. *Plants with a purpose*. Collins, London.

Treseder, N.G. & Blamey, M. 1981. *The book of Magnolias*. Collins, London.

Underwood, Mrs D. 1971. *Grey and silver plants*. Collins, London.

Booth, Raymond C.

Elick, D. & Booth, R. 1992. *Japonica magnifica*. Alan Sutton, Stroud in association with the Fine Art Society and Sagapress Inc./Timber Press Inc., OR.

Urquhart, B.L. (ed.). 1956–60. *The Camellia*. 2 volumes. Leslie Urquhart Press, Sharpthorne, Sussex.

Brasier, Jenny

Grenfell, D. 1990. *Hosta: the flowering foliage plant*. Batsford, London.

Cameron, Elizabeth

Cameron, E. 1980. *A book of white flowers*. K.D. Duval, Pitlochry.

—1982. *A Floral ABC*. Webb & Bower, Exeter.

—1983. *A wild flower alphabet*. Webb & Bower, Exeter.

Condy, G.

Henderson, L. 1995. *Plant invaders of southern Africa*. Plant Protection Research Institute, South Africa.

Coombs, Jill

Chatto, B. 1985. *Plant portraits*. J.M. Dent, London in association with the Telegraph Sunday Magazine.

Grey-Wilson, C. 1987. *Herbs for cooking and health*. Collins, London.

Mathew, B. 1982. *The crocus*. Batsford, London.

Dale, Patricia

Rohde, E.S. 1989. *The scented garden*. The Medici Society, London.

Dean, Pauline

Huxley, A. (ed.). 1992. *The new Royal Horticultural Society dictionary of gardening*. MacMillan, London and Stockton Press, NY.

Demonte Family

Ferraz Blower, C.D. 1990. *Fauna e flora do Brasil – Fauna and flora of Brazil*. Salamandra, Rio de Janeiro.

White, J.J. (comp.). 1985. *For love of nature: Brazilian flora and fauna in watercolour by Etienne, Rosália and Yvonne Demonte*. Hunt Institute, Pittsburgh and Wave Hill, NY.

Demonte, Etienne

Ruschi, A. 1979. *Aves do Brasil*, 2 volumes. Editora Rios Limitada, São Paulo.

—1980. *Beija-flores do estado do Espírito Santo*. Editora Rios Limitada, São Paulo. Published in English as *Hummingbirds in the State of Espirito Santo* by Editora Rios, São Paulo (1980).

Demonte, Yvonne

Ruschi, A. 1979. *Aves do Brasil*, 2 volumes. Editora Rios Limitada, São Paulo.

Dowden, Anne Ophelia Todd

Busch, P. 1977. *Wildflowers and the stories behind their names*. Charles Scribner's Sons, NY.

Borland, H. 1977. *The golden circle: a book of months*. Thomas Y. Crowell, NY.

—1987. *Plants of Christmas*. Thomas Y. Crowell, NY.

Crowell, R.L. 1982. *The lore and legends of flowers*. Thomas Y. Crowell, NY.

Dowden, A.O. 1963. *Look at a flower*. Thomas Y. Crowell, NY.

—1964. *The secret life of the flowers*. Odyssey Press, NY.

—& Thomson, R. 1965. *Roses*. Odyssey Press, NY.

—1972. *Wild green things in the city: a book of weeds*. Thomas Y. Crowell, NY.

—1975. *The blossom on the bough: a book of trees*.

Thomas Y. Crowell, NY (Reprinted 1994 by Tickner & Fields.)

—1978. *State flowers*. Thomas Y. Crowell, NY.

—1979. *This noble harvest: a chronicle of herbs*. Collins, NY.

—1984. *From flower to fruit*. Thomas Y. Crowell, NY. (Reprinted 1994 by Tickner & Fields.)

—1990. *The clover and the bee: a book of pollination*. Thomas Y. Crowell, NY.

—1994. *Poisons in our path: plants that harm and heal*. Thomas Y. Crowell, NY.

Kerr, J. 1969. *Shakespeare's flowers*. Thomas Y. Crowell, NY and Longmans Young Books Ltd., London.

Paterson, J. & K. 1986. *Consider the lilies: plants of the Bible*. Thomas Y. Crowell, NY.

Untermeyer, L. 1970. *Plants of the Bible*. Golden Press, NY.

Edwards, Brigid

Richards, J. 1993. *Primula*. Batsford, London and Timber Press, OR.

Farrer, Ann

*   denotes that books were illustrated under Ann Farrer's previous name of Ann Davies.

Boyce, P. 1993. *The genus Arum*. HMSO, London in association with the Royal Botanic Gardens, Kew.

Fitter, R, Fitter, A. & Farrer, A. 1984. *Collins guide to the grasses, sedges, rushes and ferns of Britain and northern Europe*. Collins, London.

*Launert, E. 1981. *The Hamlyn guide to the edible and medicinal plants of Britain and northern Europe*. Hamlyn, UK.

*Lousley, J.E. & Kent, D.H. 1981. *Docks and knotweeds of the British Isles*. BSBI Handbook No. 3, London.

*Polunin, O. 1980. *Flowers of Greece and the Balkans: a field guide*. Oxford University Press.

—& Stainton, A. 1984. *Flowers of the Himalaya*. Oxford University Press.

*Tutin, T.G. 1980. *Umbellifers of the British Isles*. BSBI Handbook No. 2, London.

Feng, Jinyong

Flora Reipublicae Popularis Sinicae. 1959–89. Volumes 1–78. Science Press, Beijing.

Iconographia Cormophytorum Sinicorum. 1972–76. Volumes 1–5. Science Press, Beijing.

Futakuchi, Yoshio

Asayama, E. 1971-74. *Ornamental plants in colour*. Volumes 1 and 2. Heibonsha, Tokyo.

Futakuchi, Y. 1992. *The picture book of Camellias*. Yasaka Book Publishing, Tokyo.

Katoh, M. 1974. *Orchids in colour*. Heibonsha, Tokyo.

Suzuki, S. & Momiyama, Y. 1983. *Roses in colour*. Heibonsha, Tokyo.

Tsuyama, T. 1986. *Camellia cultivars of Japan*. Heibonsha, Tokyo.

Grierson, Mary A.

Grierson, M., Stearn, W.T. & Brickell, C.D. 1987. *An English florilegium*. Thames & Hudson, London.

Grey-Wilson, C. 1988. *The genus Cyclamen*. Royal Botanic Gardens, Kew in association with Christopher Helm, Bromley and Timber Press, OR.

Hunt, P.F. & Grierson, M. 1973. *Orchidaceae*. The Bourton Press, Bourton, England.

Huxley, A.J. 1967. *Mountain flowers*. Blandford, London.

Mathew, B. 1982. *The crocus*. Batsford, London.

—1989. *Hellebores*. Alpine Garden Society, Woking.

Guest, Coral

Guest, C. 1992. *The Royal roses of London*. Victoria's Secret Garden, London.

Hart-Davies, Christine

Bright, H. 1989. *A year in a Victorian garden*. Pyramid, London.

Huxley, A. (ed.). 1992. *The new Royal Horticultural Society dictionary of gardening*. MacMillan, London and Stockton Press, NY.

Wright, M. 1984. *The complete handbook of garden plants*. Michael Joseph, London.

Haywood, Helen

Palmer, J. (ed.). 1991. *A garden for all seasons*. Readers Digest, London.

Imai, Mariko

The grand atlas of world plants. 1986. K.K. Hokuryukan, Tokyo.

The grand atlas of alpine flora. 1987. K.K. Hokuryukan, Tokyo.

Azuma, A. 1979. *Horticulture*. Publishing Division of Tamagawa University, Tokyo.

Koyama, T. 1979. *Flowers and trees*. Publishing Division of Tamagawa University, Tokyo.

Miyagawa, M. 1988. *Cotton*. Fukuinkanshoten, Tokyo.

Udagawa, Y. 1983–84. *The story of orchids*. K.K. Shin Kikaku, Tokyo.

—1994. *Masdevallia and Dracula*. Nigensha Publishing, Tokyo.

Irani. Jamshed Pirojshaw

Ali, S.A. & Ripley, S.D. 1983. *The handbook of the birds of India and Pakistan*. 3 volumes. Oxford University Press.

—1986. *A field guide to the birds of the eastern Himalayas*. Oxford University Press.

—1964. *The book of Indian birds*. Bombay Natural History Society

—& Futehally, L. 1967. *Common birds*. National Book Trust, New Dehli.

Ara, J. 1970. *Watching birds*. National Book Trust, New Dehli.

Chopra, U.C. 1984. *Our feathered friends*. National Book Trust, New Dehli.

Jones, Paul

Blunt, W. 1971. *Flora superba*. Tryon Gallery, London.

—1976. *Flora magnifica*. Tryon Gallery, London.

Urquhart, B.L. (ed.). 1956–60. *The Camellia*. 2 volumes. Leslie Urquhart Press, Sharpthorne, Sussex.

Waterhouse, E.G. 1947. *Camellia quest*. Ure Smith, Sydney.

—1952. *Camellia trail*. Ure Smith, Sydney.

Jowett, Jenny

Grenfell, D. & Grounds, R. 1990. *The white garden*. Crowood Press, Swindon.

Kakuta, Yoko

Hasimoto, S. 1990. *Garden farming without agrochemicals*. Ichigaya, Shinjukuku, Ienohikari Publishing Association, Tokyo.

Izawa, K. 1990. *Herb atlas in colour*. Kanda, Chiyodaku, Shufu no Tomo Co., Tokyo.

Takahashi, Y. 1990. *How to grow herbs*. Ichigaya, Shinjukuku, Ienohikari Publishing Association, Tokyo.

Tanaka, S. 1989. *Love for wild flowers*. Ichigaya, Shinjukuku, Ienohikari Publishing Association, Tokyo.

Thomas, I. & Takahashi, Y. 1990. *How to grow 65 species of herbs*. Kanda, Chiyodaku, Shufu no Tomo Co., Tokyo.

King, Christabel

Cribb, P. & Butterfield, I. 1988. *The genus Pleione*. The Royal Botanic Gardens, Kew in association with Christopher Helm, Bromley and Timber Press, OR.

Heywood, V.H. (ed.) 1978. *Flowering plants of the world*. Elsevier, Oxford and Mayflower Books, NY.

Mathew, B. 1989. *The genus Lewisia*. Royal Botanic Gardens, Kew in association with Christopher Helm, Bromley and Timber Press, OR.

Michael, P. 1980. *All good things around us*. Ernest Benn, London and Holt, Rinehart & Winston, NY.

Taylor, N.P. 1985. *The genus Echinocereus*. Royal Botanic Gardens, Kew in association with Collingridge, Middlesex.

Yeoman, G. 1989. *Africa's mountains of the moon*. Elm Tree Books, London and Universe Books, NY.

Knox, Charlotte

Davidson, A. & Knox, C. 1991. *Fruit*. Mitchell Beazley, London.

Grigson, J. 1986. *Exotic fruits and vegetables*. Jonathan Cape, London.

Kojima, Mariko

Kojima, M. 1988. *How to draw botanical art*. Nishida Publishing, Tokyo.

Langhorne, Joanna A.

Huxley, A.J. (ed.). 1992. *The new Royal Horticultural Society dictionary of gardening*. MacMillan, London and Stockton Press, NY.

Lancaster, R. 1983. *In search of the wild asparagus*. Michael Joseph/Rainbird, London.

Mathew, B. 1982. *The crocus*. Batsford, London.

Rushforth, K. 1987. *Conifers*. Croom Helm, London.

Turner, R. 1995. *Euphorbias: a gardeners' guide*. Batsford, London and Timber Press, OR.

Lee, Katie

Armour, M.C. 1994. *Orca song*. Sound Prints, CT.

Bailer, D. 1993. *Puffin's homecoming*. Sound Prints, CT.

Jay, L.A. 1995. *Sea turtle journey*. Sound Prints, CT.

Lee, K. 1994. *A visit to Galápagos.* Abrams, NY.

Lind, A. 1994. *Black bear cub.* Sound Prints, CT.

Lincoln, Thalia

Rourke, J. & Lincoln, T. *Mimetes.* Tiyan Publishers, Cape Town.

Liška, Petr

Slaba, R. 1992. *The illustrated guide to cacti.* Sterling Publishing Co., Inc., NY.

Mee, Margaret

Mayo, S. 1988. *Margaret Mee's Amazon.* Royal Botanic Gardens, Kew.

Mee, M. 1980. *Flores do Amazonas – flowers of the Amazon.* Record, Rio de Janeiro.

—1968. *Flowers of the Brazilian forests.* Tryon Gallery, London.

—(ed. T. Morrison). 1988. *In search of flowers of the Amazon forests.* Nonesuch Expeditions, Suffolk.

Megarrity, Lindsay

Megarrity, L. 1991. *Fiori.* Torsanlorenzo, Rome.

McEwen, Rory

Blunt, W. 1977. *Tulips and tulipomania.* Basilisk Press, London.

Koch, K. & McEwen, R. 1979. *From the air.* Taranman, London.

Moreton, O.C. 1955. *Old carnations and pinks.* George Rainbird in association with Collins, London.

—1964. *The auricula.* The Ariel Press, London.

Olson, George

Olson, G. 1990. *Plant studies from the American prairies.* British Museum (Natural History), London.

Pistoia, Marilena

Bianchini, F. & Corbetta, F. 1973. *I frutti della Terra.* 1973. Arnoldo Mondadori, Milan. American edition published as *The complete book of fruits and vegetables* by Crown Publishers, NY (1975). English edition published as *The fruits of the earth* by Cassell, London (1976).

—1975. *Le piante della salute.* Arnoldo Mondadori, Milan. English edition published as *The kindly fruits* by Cassell, London (1977).

Peroni, L. 1984. *Il Linguaggio dei Fiori.* Arnoldo Mondadori, Milan. English translation published as *Glorious flowers* by Arch Cape Press, NY (1990).

Reader's Digest family guide to natural medicine. 1993. Readers Digest, NY/Montreal.

Rees-Davies, Kay

Leyens, T. 1995. *Plantas endemicas e arvores indigenas de Cabo Verde.* Bonn University, Germany.

Rosser, Celia

Catcheside, D.G. 1980. *Mosses of South Australia.* Woolman, Adelaide.

Rosser, C.E. & George, A.S. *The banksias.* Volume I (1981) – Academic Press, London in association with Monash University, Clayton, Victoria; Volume II (1988) – Monash Universiry in association with the State Bank of Victoria; Volume III (in preparation).

Rust, Graham

Sackville-West, V. 1993. *Some flowers.* Pavilion, London in association with The National Trust.

Sanders, Rosanne

Rougetel, H. de 1992. *A little book of old roses.* Appletree Press, Belfast.

Sanders, R. 1988. *The English apple.* Phaidon, Oxford, in association with the RHS. American edition published as *The apple book* by The Philosophical Library, NY, (1988).

Saul, Margaret

Andrews, S.B. 1990. *Ferns of Queensland.* Queensland Department of Primary Industries, Brisbane.

Beesley, P. (ed.). 1989. *Fauna of Australia.* Volume 5 (Nautiloidea). Bureau of Flora and Fauna, Canberra.

George, A.S. & Orchard, A.E. 1981 onward. *Flora of Australia.* Australian Biological Resources Study, Canberra.

Pearn, J. 1990. *Medicine and botany, an Australian cadaster.* University of Queensland Press, Brisbane.

Stanley, T.D. & Ross, E.M. 1983–89. *Flora of south-eastern Queensland.* Volumes 1–3. Queensland Department of Primary Industries, Brisbane.

Scott, Gillian

Roberts, B. & Silcock, R. 1982, 1993. *Western grasses.* DDIP, Toowoomba, Queensland.

Sellars, Pandora

Boyce, P. 1993. *The genus Arum.* HMSO, London in association with the Royal Botanic Gardens, Kew.

Cribb, P. 1987. *The genus Paphiopedilum.* Royal Botanic Gardens, Kew in association with Collingridge, Middlesex.

Le Sueur, F. 1984. *Flora of Jersey.* Société Jersiaise, Jersey, C.I.

Singer, Alan

Buckley, V. (ed.). 1986. *State birds.* E.P. Dutton, NY.

Hornblow, A. 1991. *Birds do the strangest things.* Random House, NY.

Miles, B. 1976. *Bulbs for the home gardener.* Grosset & Dunlap, NY.

Mott, R. 1975. *The total book of house plants.* Delacorte Press, NY.

Singer, Arthur

Austin, O.L. Jr. 1961. *Birds of the world.* Golden Press, NY (new edn 1983).

Bond, J. 1974. *Birds of the West Indies.* Collins, London.

Bruun, B. 1970. *The Hamlyn guide to birds of Britain and Europe.* Hamlyn, London. American edition published as *Birds of Europe* by McGraw Hill, USA (1970).

Buckley, V. (ed.). 1986. *State birds.* E.P. Dutton, NY.

Fichter, G. 1982, 1992. *Birds of North America – a beginner's guide.* Random House, NY.

Robbins, C.S. Bruun, B. & Zim, H. 1966. *Birds of North America – a guide to field identification.* Golden Press, NY.

Stones, Margaret

Cox, E.M.H. & P.A. *Modern rhododendrons* (1956); *Modern shrubs* (1958); *Modern trees* (1961). Nelson, Edinburgh.

Cox, P.A. 1973. *Dwarf rhododendrons.* Batsford, London in association with the RHS.

—1979. *The larger species of Rhododendron.* Batsford, London.

—1985. *The smaller rhododendrons.* Batsford, London.

Curtis, W. 1967–78. *The endemic flora of Tasmania.* 6 volumes. Ariel Press, London.

Mathew, B. 1982. *The crocus.* Batsford, London.

Stern, F.C. 1956. *Snowdrops and snowflakes.* RHS, London.

Stones, M. & Urbatsch, L. 1991. *Flora of Louisiana.* Louisiana State University Press, Baton Rouge and London.

Turrill, W.T. 1960–62. *A supplement to Elwes' Monograph of the genus Lilium.* 2 parts. RHS, London.

Tcherepnine, Jessica

Mawson, T. 1994. *The garden room.* Clarkson N. Potter, NY.

Toyota, Michiko

The grand atlas of alpine flora. 1987. K.K. Hokuryukan, Tokyo.

Uchijo, Yoko

Akane colour atlas for children. 1980. Volumes 5, 6, 7. Nishikanda, Chiyodaku, Akane Publishing, Tokyo.

Takahashi, K. 1978. *Uncle bear and acorn.* Ichigayadaimachi, Shinjukuku, Komine Publishing, Tokyo.

Ward-Hilhorst, Ellaphie

van der Walt, J.J.A. 1977. *Pelargoniums of southern Africa.* Purnell & Sons, Cape Town.

—& Vorster, P.J. 1981. *Pelargoniums of southern Africa.* Volume 2. Juta, Kenwyn.

—&— 1988. *Pelargoniums of southern Africa.* Volume 3. National Botanic Gardens, Kirstenbosch.

van Jaarsveld, E.J. 1994. *Gasterias of South Africa.* Fernwood Press, Vlaeberg in association with the National Botanical Institute.

Wunderlich, Eleanor B.

Reader's Digest family guide to natural medicine. 1993. Readers Digest, NY/Montreal.

Wunderlich, E.B. 1991. *Botanical illustration in watercolor.* Watson-Guptill Publications, NY. English edition published as *Botanical illustration watercolour technique* by Studio Vista, London (1991).

Zhang, Tai-li

Flora Reipublicae Popularis Sinicae. 1959–89. Volumes 7, 15, 16, 17, 28. Science Press, Beijing.

Illustrated flora of China. Beijing.